TRANCE AND TRAUMA

A Recovery Manual for P.T.S.D. Therapists, Veterans and their Families

Michael McGee, LPC, MA, DCH

ISBN: 978-1-929661-35-0
Library of Congress Control Number: 2010934739
Unattributed quotations are by Michael McGee

Cover Design by Allen Chips and Blake Courtenay Moore
First printing, first edition: October, 2010

Transpersonal Publishing, div. AHU,LLC
PO Box 7220, Kill Devil Hills, NC 27948
www.TranspersonalPublishing.com
800-296-MIND

Transpersonal Publishing is a "green publisher." Most books are printed on recycled paper (look for the recycle symbol on the cover). All titles and distributed lines are available at special quantity discounts for bulk purchases for conferences/conventions, fund-raising, and educational or institutional use. For details, contact the publisher.

Authors seeking a publisher must submit query letters by e-mail to have their work considered, and only through the submission guidelines on the website.

Orders:
Email: Orders@holistictree.com
Wholesale—www.TranspersonalPublishing.com; or phone the publisher
Retail—www.Holistictree.com; go to the online shopping cart

Printed in the USA on FSC certified, recycled paper.

To Mom:

Peggy Siner McGee
February 10, 1932 – September 6, 2008
A Mother's faith never falters.

I am very grateful to my family for believing in me, tolerating long hours, and enduring restless days. Thank you to Sarah, Amanda, Jacob, and Dad for all of your support. Special thanks to Allen and Dee Chips for making a dream become a reality. Also, I greatly appreciate the editorial assistance of Theresa Burriss, a true lifesaver.

CONTENTS

"We sleep safe in our beds because rough men stand ready in the night to visit violence on those who would do us harm."

---George Orwell on a BBC broadcast, April 4, 1942

Introduction

It has been said that human history is written in blood. If that is so, how could we not suffer the fearful stress resulting from such an existence? The majority of human beings seem to live in a culture of war and fear. There are armed conflicts right now on 4 continents. The United States lists 42 known terrorist organizations world wide. If we talk about a history of blood, all we need do is look at the history of these United States. Our country had a violent birth in revolution. It has continued on a violent path since birth. There has been one war after another over the years, including a terrible civil war that still is recorded in the wounded psyche of our nation. War has been ingrained into our conscious and unconscious mind. We might simply observe this by looking at our expressions. We have so many wars in our language: a war on drugs, a war on poverty, a war on cancer, and a war on terrorism. We seem to declare wars easily on anything that appears to cause us difficulty. It is a reality that flows into our consciousness like a poison spring.

But, it is not just our country or our time that is exposed to these horrors. Human history seems to move from one war to another. We are exposed to an endless parade of war. The parade of death invades our thoughts. Each of these thoughts and ideas create a ripple in our brains of neural connections to violence and fear. Like thousands of tiny streams, these ripples flow slowly together. As more of these thoughts occupy our minds, the flow becomes a river, then, a torrent. A raging ocean of fear, anger, and violence can be the result.

Trauma is fast becoming the new epidemic of our time. Many among us claim daily that tragedy, epidemic, and disaster are on the way. Fear has become the watch word of our current leaders. But, as we enter the new era of the "War on Terror", it appears we may have opened a modern version of Pandora's Box and all that we find within is an ancient disorder of terrible consequences. The consequences of war are trauma. The consequences of a war culture will most likely become trauma. The more ambiguous the threat and the safety are, the more traumatic the results.

Recently, I attended an American Society of Clinical Hypnosis training where trauma, particularly psychological trauma, was declared by one presenter as a new epidemic. In fact, epidemiological studies indicate that 25 – 50% of U.S. Citizens are exposed to psychological trauma at some point in their lives (Acierno, Kilpatrick, & Resnick, 1999). This idea of epidemic trauma resonated with me. One could make the serious argument that merely watching the news could lead to trauma. War, violence, murder, rape, sexual abuse, and child abuse are all exposed. And, they all find entrance to our psyche, even if we are not the victims.

In approaching this work, I thought deeply about the idea of epidemic trauma. In some ways, it drew me into a shadow realm of the psyche where the possibility of darkness and secrets are found beneath the cobwebs of forgetfulness. Freud would have called this place the unconscious. The realm of consciousness we allegedly avoid at all costs. It is a place that might be within us all, especially being exposed to our cultural messages. A contemporary of Freud, the famous psychologist, Carl Jung, had dubbed this realm the"Shadow". This seems indeed a fitting name. Jung believed we had an individual and collective part of our unconscious. Therefore, our personal shadows (I will use plural instead of singular) may also connect to the collective unconscious of all shadows. This could be a domain of shadows where all of the darkness of human suffering resides. Just outside of our awareness, the memories of horror and pain from time immemorial wait terrible and traumatic events that have built their shadows through recorded history. Now, as we enter a new millennium, we too shall add to the darkness. This may appear somewhat dramatic. Of course, it is. The reality of evils done need no introduction, for suffering and trauma are part of the human drama. In our lives, this drama appears to be without end for now.

Why do I write this book? Maybe the reader is familiar with the saying,"Once a Marine, always a Marine". I volunteered for the Marine Corps in 1978. I dropped out of college to do so. There is nothing like the training of Marine Boot Camp as far as instilling a sense of duty, pride, honor, and belonging. I did not see combat. For that, I am both disappointed and grateful. I can remember the Iran Hostage crisis and how my fellow Marines and I waited and wanted so badly to go. We were determined to rescue the hostages, to kill Iranians, and restore America's honor. A small group went into a desert storm and the rest of us heard of their failure. It was a very discouraging time. Even though I had not seen combat, I did see death while in the Marine Corps. I have my memories and I still want to help. I want to aid the sons and daughters of our country who are held hostage to the memories of war.

When I was young, I always enjoyed frightening movies. The ability to suspend belief while entering that frightening space, to be thrilled by make-believe terror, and to return safely back to reality as one departs the theater is powerfully exciting. Safely, we return to our every day way of life. Don't we? But what of those poor souls who enter horrors in their day to day lives and have no theater from which to exit from? How many of us experience trauma in our daily existence with no escape? Just watch the news and observe the number of reports on incidents that must result in trauma for many involved. What of the American troops who are traumatized again and again in combat zones, safe zones, and even the "Green" zones (that have just experienced a mortar attack as I write this today)? This is not fiction. This is life as we know it. This current, particular epidemic we will be facing is the direct result of our current military operations. Three areas in particular call for our attention. They are Operation Iraqi Freedom (OIF), Operation Enduring Freedom (OEF), and the "War on Terror", or, as I like to describe it, the War of Terror. Why? Because the War of Terror implies that terrorism is a two-way war. The traumas are not limited to combatants and go both ways. I believe this to be a more accurate description.

Our current conflicts are different from previous military operations-in that we have a large volunteer force. The days of being required to go to war by the draft ended with the Vietnam Conflict, though the system of selective service remains intact for the future. Many of the troops now serving are reservists. It is possible that some of them might never have considered that they would actually go to war, but that is not the same as being drafted. Many feel-that one should be prepared to go to war-if one volunteers. I argue, that this is not relevant when the person is exposed to the truth and gore of war.

A major concern at this time is the sheer number of our men and women who are returning from war. Therefore, in this book, I want to focus on our veterans. At the time of this writing, we estimate that over 50,000 returning Veterans are experiencing Post Traumatic Stress Disorder. Some estimates I have seen indicate we may have as many as 700,000 cases by the time all of our troops return, depending on how long the war continues and how many persons have served.

In terms of verifiable statistics, as of March 20, 2009, the official U.S. casualties in Iraq (OIF) were: 4,261 US troops killed, 3425 by hostile fire, 836 by "friendly fire" or non-hostile reasons (Department of Defense, 2009). The official U.S. casualties in Afghanistan (OEF) were: 663 US troops killed, 443 by hostile fire, 220 by "friendly fire" or non-hostile means (DoD). Of these casualties, 82% were Army, 11% Marines, 3% Navy, and 4% Air Force (DoD). Also, for all these casualties: 98% were male, 90% non-officers, 80% active duty, and 12% National Guard (DoD). Ethnically, these casualties were 75% Caucasian, 10% African-American, and 11% Latino (DoD). Of these, 18% were killed by non-hostile causes, 51% of U.S. casualties were under 25 years of age, and 70% were from the U.S. Army (DoD). The total number of U.S. Troops wounded at this time is 33,476 (DoD). According to the Army Office of the Surgeon General, between September 2001 and January 12, 2009, there were 1,286 amputations in OIF, OEF, and unaffiliated conflicts. The total includes 935 major limb amputations and 351 minor amputations. Of these wounded, 20% were serious brain or spinal injuries (this total excludes psychological injuries such as PTSD). The Military Mental health System indicates 43,779 patients have been diagnosed with a traumatic brain injury (TBI) in calendar years 2003 through 2007. The MHS also indicates that 39,365 patients have been diagnosed with PTSD. As for U.S. Troops in need of mental health services, it appears that 30% develop serious mental health issues within three to four months of returning home. In terms of trauma exposure, 92% of our troops report being attacked or ambushed, 94.5% have been required to seek and/or find dead bodies, 95 % have been fired upon, and 86.5% saw and/or know someone who was seriously injured or killed (Department of Defense, 2008). Mental health issues appear to be reported at all time highs for this population. Recent statistics have indicated a total increase of over 100,000 diagnosable mental disorders. Suicides have shown a marked increase (US Army release 1/29/09). In January 2009 alone, 24 soldiers are believed to have committed suicide. This number is six times greater than those who killed themselves in January 2008 (CNN 2/5/09). In fact, Army records indicated an eleven percent increase in suicides in 2008. This was an all time high for suicides of Army personnel since 1980. As of March 2009, 177 service members in Iraq and 29 in Afghanistan have died of self-inflicted wounds (Department of Defense, 2009). This historic high equals a rate of 20 suicides per 100,000 for the U.S. Army. At this time, it seems that our Veteran's Administration is poorly funded and poorly prepared to deal with this epidemic.

Large numbers of veterans have experienced the shadows of war that might make very strong impressions on any person. Our beloved sons and daughters, the men and women of the United States military, are coming home. Some are already here, some are in transit, and eventually, all will return. They are the survivors of war. With each of them, they will carry shadows. Some will be small and easily forgotten. Many-will not be forgotten, and in many ways, shapes, or forms-demand the attention of those who would rather forget. This book is my attempt to help. For each of us here, the task to help is ahead. Hopefully, we shall be the guides who travel by their side into the minds of shadow while assisting them to emerge in wholeness and light. We must be the focus or compass-on their passage home.

Writing this book has also been a personal journey through the past and present. It seems that just being a part of the military leaves a permanent mark on one's psyche. I did not know how much until this work began. I have felt the pain-of myself, clients, and veterans (from all sources) real, subjective, and empathetic. I had no idea...how profound the effects of my short tour in the Marines had been-before beginning this work. In this writing, there have been triggers for me that served as cues or reminders of experiences long forgotten in my conscious mind. They serve as a bridge between myself and those I have assisted on this journey. There is a connection of service between all members of the Armed Forces. Many feelings are shared both in peace and war. In the Greek myths, many enter into the realm of Hades. Some... brave souls-return. Their knowledge, must be shared-to help those who follow-to return home, too.

This book is written primarily for the more advanced practitioner of hypnosis and therapy. If you have little training in hypnosis, or if you are not a professional therapist, there is vital information that you will need to be aware of before using these techniques. I strongly suggest that any person attempting to use these methods have an advanced education in counseling, psychology, social work, or medicine. Then, it is very important to receive a basic hypnosis certification or training from one of the various professional hypnosis organizations. There are many resources for this training available. I recommend the National Association of Transpersonal Hypnotherapists (NATH) or the American Society of Clinical Hypnosis (ASCH) for a firm foundation in this work.

This book is my attempt to focus on the traumas of war and how hypnosis might be used as an effective therapy to help eliminate this epidemic. In so doing, I am hopeful that many of our suffering veterans will return to productive lives, where they leave the horrors of war behind them. At the least, I am optimistic that many will be able to reduce their symptoms resulting from trauma-and move on. This new epidemic is currently a slow moving wave of fear that will continue to grow. The crest is not yet in sight. It is important to remember-as you read, that hypnotherapy is not the only method, that is effective-in the treatment of Post Traumatic Stress. There are other paths to wholeness available. Whatever path is chosen for persons who suffer the distress of PTSD, they must travel it to its final destination-to be free. It is best they have assistance on the way. We must do what we can-to be that assistance-with compassion, courage, and empathy. The darkness of Hades-can shadow the honor a warrior merits...the self respect the survivor deserves when coming home. As therapists, we will aid in bringing the darkness into the light. In the light, the shadows of the past can be defined, integrated, and healed. The return from darkness-can be completed. The warrior can be fully home, both within and without. This we do for the good of all concerned.

"We look back and we forget to look around"

– James Hillman

Chapter 1

History of Post Traumatic Stress Disorder

It is most likely that Post Traumatic Stress has been around since the beginning of human existence in some form or another. This is not a new phenomenon or experience. Just as war is not new to us, trauma is not new to us either. Prior to our armed conflicts, there was always the possibility of being exposed to attack by predator or deathly results from natural disasters.

The recorded history of humankind is full of tales about war and glory. We even have Gods and Goddesses of war. Whether appearing as Ares, Athena, Mars, Tyr, Kartikeya, Gun, Camaxtli, Badb, Bishamon, or many other guises, the deities of war have a strong international presence in human history. Just as "war" has been identified by many names for a long, long time, so has Post Traumatic Stress Disorder. If we look back on some of the classic works by authors and poets from days gone by, we can find evidence of PTSD. One may observe in Homer's *Iliad* and *Odyssey* that Achilles and Odysseus appear to have what we would now call PTSD. Their names imply the stress that they carry with them and expose others to. For instance, Achilles may be translated as "he whose host of fighting men have grief" (Nagy, 1979). The mythological significance of this disorder presented in the warrior archetypes and these Greek tragedies is of great importance to approaching the disorder from a transpersonal perspective.

In the story of the *Iliad,* Achilles is both insulted and embarrassed by his commander's behavior. These feelings seem to exacerbate the effects of Post Traumatic Stress in this story. Achilles' prize of victory is taken from him and he is angered to the point of leaving battle for good. Similar effects played out in many instances during the Vietnam conflict as commanding officers were continually rotated in and out leading to a lack of trust in leadership. How great is this effect in OIF or OEF? In these conflicts, our troops may find that the reasons for being in Iraq were based on misinformation or that their equipment is inferior and does not offer them protection as was the case when the war in Iraq began. The troops in OIF and OEF found they had improper body armor, improperly armored vehicles, and leaders back home that did not seem to care. According to Shay (1994), this greatly increases the risks of PTSD.

Shay (2002) also considers the story of Ulysses in the *Odyssey,* and the effects of returning home on the hardened combat veteran. The warrior finds himself interacting with those who have not had the experience of being in a battle where death is hovering continuously to snatch away one's self or comrades and wonders at the difference between that experience and those mere mortals who remained in their comfortable lives. Our veteran knows how easy it is to die or kill in that other world, that world that appears to have not been left behind but come along as part of the psyche. It may be discovered that even though the battles were left behind, anxiety is now a constant companion.

PTSD was recognized by many writers from the past. Shakespeare appears to have multiple characters who suffered from it. For instance, in Shakespeare's *Henry IV,* Lady Perce says to her husband, Hotspur,

"In thy faint slumbers I by thee have watch'd, and heard thee murmur tales of iron wars; Speak terms of manage to thy bounding steed; Cry "Courage! To the field!" And thou hast talked of sallies and retires; of trenches, tents; Of palisadoes, frontiers, parapets, Of basilisks, of cannon, culverin, Or prisoner's ransom, and of soldiers slain, And all the current of a heady fight. Thy spirit within thee hath been so at war, And thus hath so bestir'd thee in thy sleep, That beads of sweat have stood upon thy brow, Like bubbles in a late-disturbed stream: And in thy face strange motions have appear'd, Such as we see when men restrain their breath On some great sudden haste. O, what portents are these?"

These re-experiencing symptoms through dreams, insomnia, anxiety, depression, and symptoms of physical distress are most certainly those of PTSD (Matsakis, 1994).

As quoted above and in other stories, there have been a number of ways people have attempted to comprehend or explain the fact that undetectable injuries from exposure to war zone stress; no visible wounds, no bleeding, no broken bones could produce, at times, incapacitating problems. However, we must return to more current times, such as the late 19th century, both in Europe and the United States, when medical and mental health practitioners began to take notice of the impact of traumatic stress, war zone-, or combat-stress.

In the United States, medical knowledge of PTSD is recorded from the American Civil War (Pizarro, Silver, & Prause, 2006). In the Civil War, it was often thought that war trauma was related to the idea of nostalgia. For instance, the reason why a young troop from Vermont was having trouble was because he was homesick for being back in the Green Mountains, while he was fighting in Georgia or along the Mississippi River near Vicksburg. There are recorded findings related to Civil War Veterans that indicate the physical and mental health costs of traumatic war experiences were very high (Pizarro, Silver, & Prause).

Traumatic reactions in the late 19th Century were labeled many ways. Some of these reactions included medical/ neurological explanations, hypotheses, and models such as, Soldier's heart, Buried Alive Syndrome, Da Costa syndrome, and neuron-circulatory asthenia. These diagnoses focused on possibly altered cardiovascular function, assumed to be a result of combat stress. At this time, there was also a neurological model used to explain these problems. This was a civilian counterpart labeled as "Railway Spine". This label referred to people who had been in train accidents in the late 19th century and were incapacitated despite no identifiable physical injury. Also, there were psychiatric models that were used as attempted explanations. In Europe, Schreck neurosis, or fright neurosis, was a prominent psychological model. The idea being that exposure to situations that elicit extreme fright produced continued anxiety. Gross Stress Reaction, which appears to be the first use of the word stress for this disorder, was recorded in the first Diagnostic and Statistical Manual for Mental Disorders. This description was removed in the later revised DSM II. Afterwards, the description became Combat Fatigue or Combat Exhaustion, which is a part psychological and part physical problem. And finally, the name given to the psychoanalytic understanding of the difficulties that happened to people after experiences in a war zone was recorded as War Neurosis.

The psychoanalysts in Europe, such as Freud, Breuer, and Forensier, noticed altered psychological functioning among German and Austrian soldiers involved in the Franco-

Prussian War, the War of 1870, and World War I. A neurological explanation that came out of the First World War for these injuries is called "Shell-shock". The theory was that experiencing the blasts of big artillery guns used in trench warfare somehow damaged or disconnected the neuronal connections in the brain. An estimated 80,000 soldiers were treated for this psychological trauma at that time. It's kind of paradoxical that in the current wars in Iraq and Afghanistan, we have a genuinely identifiable physical shell-shock. It is called traumatic brain injury and without a doubt, many people who have traumatic brain injury also have PTSD, but this will be discussed later.

In 1918, Freud wrote about the phenomenon of "War Neurosis" as a conflict between the soldier's old peaceful ego and the new warlike ego where the peaceful ego fears losing its life as a result of the actions of its "parasitic double" (Freud & Horowtiz, 1999). He further indicated that he did not believe mercenaries or professional soldiers could suffer from war neurosis because their primary ego state was war-like and produced no conflict. However, those who did not prepare for combat experiences or were conscripted to fight (not volunteers) would suffer greatly from the experience.

Freud also found that painful electric shock therapy, developed by Julius von Wagner-Jauregg in Vienna, produced short term symptom removal (Freud, 1972). These subjects were then returned to the front lines where they relapsed very quickly. This was obviously not a long term solution. Freud suggested that the only lasting cure for this neurosis came from psychoanalysis. Freud also wrote that as the war ended, so did war neurosis. We know that this is erroneous based on today's veteran population.

A contemporary of Freud, Carl Jung, also wrote of the phenomenon of "War Neurosis" and "Abreaction" (Jung, 1966). Jung appeared to believe that traumatic neurosis would often result if there was something already amiss within the psyche prior to being exposed to the trauma. If this was the case, he did not seem to believe that the neurosis was specifically caused by trauma. Jung believed that we all experience trauma in order to know the soul and give our lives meaning. However, he distinguished another separate form of trauma that appeared to be a result of war. Therefore, he was the first to recommend that war trauma neurosis might need to be treated differently than a pre-war existing condition or predisposition to neurotic behaviors. He believed that for some people, the emotionally charged state that occurred following exposure to trauma took on a life of its own as a complex within the psyche. He likened this to a "psychic wound" which when irritated by any incoming information, reactivates the same emotional charge creating a "regular emotional explosion" within the person's psyche (Jung). This would explain the powerful reactivation or reliving of the emotional event. Jung went further in reporting that the abreaction (emotional reaction to the past event) and the dramatic rehearsal and emotional recapitulation, whether in hypnosis or the waking state, were often beneficial to the patient (1966). However, Jung goes further in stating that abreaction alone does not work in all cases and in some may be harmful. If abreaction alone was needed, then the patients could just relive the emotions and cure themselves. This does not work in many cases. The therapist plays an essential role. Jung believed that the most important factor is to remove the dissociation from the traumatic event and therefore reintegrate the complex into the psyche. The end result is a "whole" person. This will be addressed completely in the discussion concerning treatment.

In the 1940s to 1980s, many of what we would now call post traumatic type reactions began to be described in the literature. Watkins (1949) wrote an excellent volume on the hypnotic treatment of"war neurosis". This appears to be the first exclusive examination of the many uses for hypnosis in treating this population. Possibly, this is the beginning of increased recognition or the beginning of our current epidemic. Though there is quite a bit of speculation about what may have changed during this time, increased recognition is most likely a large factor. Basically, these post traumatic reactions were named by the character of the traumatic stress that occurred. Therefore, we had rape trauma syndrome; survivor syndrome, not just for military persons, but also for survivors of concentration camps; war neurosis; shell shock; and post-Vietnam syndrome, which was the term used in the '60s and '70s, when veterans from Vietnam first came home and sought treatment.

The history of post traumatic stress diagnosis starts in 1980 with the American Psychiatric Association's third edition of its Diagnostics and Statistical Manual; the DSM-III. This is the first time that PTSD, by the name of PTSD, became established as a diagnosis. The stressor norm was that people had to have been exposed to a"recognizable stressor that would evoke significant symptoms of distress in almost anyone." The DSM-III had three symptom clusters based on clinical experience and on models that Harowitz had been developing. There was a **re-experiencing** cluster of symptoms. There was a **numbing** cluster, and **changes in personality** appearing as an assortment of 12 other symptoms in the original DSM III. So, the three symptom clusters (based on clinical experience) were: **re-experiencing, numbing and** detachment, and changes in personality.

In 1987, the DSM-III was revised to the DSM-III-R, which included some important changes to the PTSD diagnosis. A traumatic event was defined as **"an event outside the range of usual human experience"** that would be **"markedly distressing to almost anyone."** This occurred in the late '80s (1987) and the belief was that traumatic events were "outside the range of normal human experience." Recently, we have found that this isn't the case. As is a theme of this writing, trauma is now found in almost epidemic proportions in the United States, a country internally mostly at peace. We now find that more than 60% of all adult men and women in this country will have been exposed to at least one traumatic stressor in their lives. Since that time, we know that traumatic events are NOT outside the range of normal human experience. Also, during this period, avoidance and numbing symptoms were paired together.

The DSM-III-R expanded the number of symptoms from 12 to 17. Also, the duration and onset criteria were added to the diagnosis. PTSD had to endure over a time period. An individual couldn't have PTSD in less than a month from the time of the event. Thirty days had to elapse to give time for normal adaptive functioning to start to happen. As I previously mentioned, it has been discovered that traumatic exposure is not outside the range of normal human experience. The DSM-III did not allow for the fact that for some people an event might be traumatic and for other, more resilient people, the same event might not be at all traumatic. The whole issue of individual differences was left to be addressed at a later time by the DSM-IV and DSM-IV-TR.

In the DSM-IV, the stressor condition was expanded

to become composed of two sections. One, a person had to experience, witness, or be confronted by the death or serious injury to self or others. This is definitely not outside of the range of human experience. Therefore, because it is no longer something outside the range of normal human experience, the number of persons who could possibly fit in this diagnostic category is greater than before. This is an important change since it expands and individualizes the diagnosis. Because of this, individual differences now play a greater role in determining a diagnosis. Further, it was no longer just a matter of having been in the wrong place at the wrong time and experiencing the event. Also, the potential client must have had an intense emotional response to the event. Finally, in the DSM-IV-TR, the emotional reaction is more distinctly defined. It is characterized as responding with intense fear, helplessness, and horror.

However, the DSM–IV essentially kept the three symptom clusters that were in the DSM III: the re-experiencing, the avoidance/numbing, and the hyper-arousal symptoms. The potential client had to have these symptoms and the onset had to persist at least a month beyond their original exposure to the traumatic experience. And finally, another additional finding in the DSM-IV for a condition that must be met was the F criterion. Beginning with the DSM–IV, this condition must be met in all potential psychiatric diagnoses, that is; in addition to having the symptoms themselves, these symptoms **had to be incapacitating.** They must cause significant distress or impairment of functioning. This brings us to our current understanding and diagnosis as it stands today.

"What is now proved was once only imagined"

– William Blake

Chapter 2

Current Diagnostic Criteria for Post Traumatic Stress Disorder

The diagnostic criteria for Post Traumatic Stress Disorder (PTSD) as reported in the current Diagnostic and Statistical Manual of Mental Disorders, 4th Edition, Text Revision (DSM-IV-TR; APA, 2000) is that PTSD is an anxiety disorder which may develop in the aftermath of an event that is experienced or witnessed and involves actual or perceived threat to life or physical integrity. Also, the person's emotional reaction to the event is characterized by horror, terror, or helplessness. Finally, three clusters of symptoms characterize PTSD: re-experiencing, avoidance, and hyper-arousal.

The person must have been exposed to a traumatic event. It must involve actual or threatened death, serious injury, or threat to physical integrity to self or others. The person must experience intense fear, horror, or helplessness as a result. And, there are three symptom clusters that occur within the PTSD diagnosis that must be met to confirm the diagnosis. Remember, these also occur in Acute Stress Disorder, which is experienced only for the first month following the traumatic event.

The first cluster is the continual re-experiencing cluster in which you persistently have one of the following symptoms:

- recurrent and intrusive distressing recollections of

event

- recurrent distressing dreams of event
- acting as if or feeling the event was recurring
- psychological distress at cues resembling or symbolizing the event
- physiological reactivity to cues resembling or symbolizing the event

For this category, it is important to repeat that a person only needs to report experiencing one of the symptoms. Clients meet this requirement if they are suffering from recurrent distressing recollections of the event when awake, distressing nightmares while they're asleep, flashbacks of the event (acting or feeling as if the event was reoccurring), or reacting to environmental cues or the stimulus-driven aspects of PTSD. A client reporting any one of these experiences has met this requirement.

If therapists will recall theories of classical conditioning from basic behavioral psychology, they will find that as in no other psychiatric diagnosis, except perhaps the diagnosis of simple phobia, the stimulus response theories of behavioral psychology are highly in evidence here. Thus, one of the prevailing theories about PTSD is that it is a classically conditioned fright response. Remember that exposure to trauma-related and similar stimuli (generalization) can induce either psychological distress or physiological reactivity. Therefore, it is possible to produce PTSD symptoms in the laboratory by exposing people to trauma cues and assessing them physiologically by looking at their brain imaging, how cerebral blood flow reacts, what areas of the brain become active or which do not, and the person's emotional reactions. This is very important in determining mind/body reactions within PTSD.

In hypnosis, we can take advantage of these stimulus-related factors of PTSD in treatment. In fact, prolonged hypnosis facilitated exposure can be related to an extinction model, in which the person experiencing PTSD is exposed repeatedly to trauma-related stimuli within the framework of a safe therapeutic environment to extinguish the post traumatic reactions. The symptoms may indeed dissipate as a result of habituation and distress reduction. **This is very important.**

The next cluster actually consists of two different components: Avoidance symptoms and numbing symptoms. As therapists, we would need to observe or identify three of these symptoms to match the diagnostic criteria for PTSD. This cluster involves avoidance of thoughts, feelings, or even talking about the event. Avoidance can lead to a very restrictive lifestyle, where in the extreme one might prefer to never leave home. You might imagine how difficult life would become and how normal functioning might become non-existent when avoidance is taken to extremes. Cognitively, when persons suffering with PTSD start having these thoughts, they often try to do something (anything) else to stop the thoughts from occurring or inhibiting them. For example, they might listen to (loud) music, or turn on the television, or attempt to find various ways to keep themselves so busy that they don't have to think about these things. They might often avoid activities or places that might be reminders of the trauma. Those are actions or behavior responses of avoidance. For example, an OIF veteran could avoid going to the beach because the sand has become a reminder of the desert. Perhaps a person who has been in an accident might avoid the site of the accident. A person who has been exposed to life threatening trauma will avoid similar environments or settings that are similar in nature to where the activating event occurred. Here, they may also experience a kind of psychic amnesia or inability to recall all or part of the trauma. And though this appears protective, the memory must be recalled in order to be integrated or allowed to fade as most memories eventually do.

Psychologically, those suffering from PTSD may experience a type of psychic numbing or a limited range of emotions, basically restricting their capacity to respond emotionally to any stimulus. This might lead to reduced interest in activities that were previously found to be exciting or pleasing. They may begin to avoid contact with other people. Do not confuse this with the loss of interest associated with depression. Generally, a depressed person has extreme negative emotional affect and not emotional numbing. This emotional numbing can be adaptive if a person is trying to eliminate the anger, anxiety, fear, guilt, and/or shame that have been interfering with day to day functioning. This may indeed be how some clients have adapted to extreme emotional stress. However, it is not adaptive and will become problematic if they are also limiting the capacity to feel positive emotions such as happiness, joy, or love. This is why persons experiencing PTSD often suffer further major casualties among their relationships, families, and marriages.

Finally, the client with PTSD may have the sense of a shortened lifespan or limited future. Sometimes, PTSD troubled people may believe that they're not going to live a normal life span. They may believe that their days are numbered. They might decide that the death they did not receive in time of war is moving quickly to catch up to them. There is no escape. So these are the seven different symptoms of the C cluster *(DSM-IV-TR)*. If a client reports or demonstrates that they have three of the symptoms listed below, they have met diagnostic criteria for PTSD.

- efforts to avoid thoughts, feelings, or conversations about the event
- efforts to avoid activities, places, or people that cause reminders
- inability to recall part of the trauma
- decreased interest or participation in activities
- feeling alienated or detached (estranged) from others
- restricted range of affect (unable to feel emotions)
- sense of foreshortened future

The final cluster of symptoms is the increased or hyper aroused cluster. A person must demonstrate or report at least two of the symptoms. These symptoms at a glance appear to be comparable to various other anxiety disorders. They are difficulty falling or staying asleep; irritability or outbursts of anger; difficulties in concentration (because the mind is wandering, somewhere else, or continuing to return to the traumatic thoughts, images, or emotions.); hyper-vigilance; and an exaggerated startle response. The exaggerated startle response is a physiological reaction that could be measured if necessary for a diagnosis. However, hyper-vigilance is more distinctive to PTSD than to other anxiety disorders. PTSD has a lot to do with safety from danger. People who have PTSD are very apprehensive about personal safety and security. They are constantly on the lookout to be certain they're not going to go through another traumatic event or situation. They deeply fear and avoid entering into a place where they're vulnerable, powerless to respond, or unable to protect themselves and/or others they care about. Often, when veterans suffering from PTSD are in the presence of those they care for these symptoms may even increase as their feeling of responsibility for the safety of others increases. This can be very upsetting. Therefore, the symptoms of increased arousal and vigilance are very important as criteria for symptoms of PTSD. Finally, remember that as therapists we need to recognize at least <u>two</u> of these symptoms for the diagnosis of PTSD.

- difficulty falling asleep or maintaining sleep
- irritability or outbursts of anger
- difficulty concentrating
- hyper-vigilance
- exaggerated startle response

At this point, I believe it is significant to note that **<u>only</u>** acute stress disorder and post traumatic stress disorder are directly linked to external events by the DSM-IV-TR. This is important enough to repeat. <u>ASD and PTSD are the only mental disorders linked to external events</u>. No other disorders in the text share this distinction. This recognizes that when exposed to enough stress, any person has the potential for stress associated dis-ease. Also, it is significant that as a result of this, we practitioners are acknowledging that any human may experience a stress related dis-ease when their exposure to stressful events goes beyond

their capability to cope with the experience.

"Trouble? Life is trouble! Only death is nice. To live is to roll up your sleeves and embrace trouble"

– Zorba the Greek

Chapter 3

Prevalence of Trauma

At this point, I would like to briefly describe the prevalence of trauma and PTSD. As reported earlier, trauma is near epidemic in our society. The National Comorbidity Survey indicates that traumatic experiences seem to occur quite often with more than 60% of the population of the United States reporting that they have experienced a traumatic event in their lives (Kessler, Sonnega, Bromer, Hughes, & Nelson, 1995). If you go to a country experiencing war or internal conflict like Iraq, that number often increases to over 90%. It is estimated that most all Iraqi adults have now been exposed to at least one traumatic event in their life. And in the United States, more than 25% of adults have experienced more than one traumatic event (Kessler, et al).

So, if we examine the prevalence of trauma, as reported by Kessler, et al. (1995), the most prevalent is to have witnessed a traumatic event (26%). That is, most persons are observers of trauma and not to have been affected themselves. However, of those witnesses only about 15% experienced PTSD symptoms. Next, many who experience trauma have been involved in some type of accident. About 18% of Americans have been in an accident that qualifies as a traumatic event but only about 16% of them experience PTSD symptoms. Child abuse is relatively rare as well (about 4%), as is the experience of combat (about 7%) compared to witnessing. Yet, approximately 30% of both child abuse victims and combat veterans reported PTSD symptoms. At the lower end of the trauma experience spectrum, in terms of the probability, is rape. Rape is a relatively rare event with only about 4% of Americans reporting that terrible experience. Yet, of those victims of rape, almost 50% experience PTSD symptoms (Kessler, et al. 1995). As reported before, over 50% of Americans have experienced a traumatic event in their lives. If you go to a country at war such as a conflict like OIF or OEF, that statistic most likely increases to about 95%. In countries at war, almost all adults may have been exposed to at least one traumatic event in their life. Remember, only about 25% of Americans have experienced more than 1 traumatic event.

I would like to indicate here that all trauma does not seem to be equally harmful psychologically. There is something very interesting to note here, that is, if you examine the prevalence of PTSD reported above, you can see an apparent inverse relationship. For instance, rape is the least experienced and yet seems to be the most noxious traumatic episode. Therefore, if persons are victims of rape, they are much more likely to develop PTSD than if they've witnessed a traumatic event happening to others. This is something to keep in mind when assessing PTSD. **All traumatic events are not equal in the likelihood of causing PTSD**.

Our focus here is the trauma of combat exposure. This will be a prominent concern for hypnotherapists and mental health practitioners (especially those who work within the Department of Veterans' Affairs) both now and in the future as more veterans return from OIF and OEF. However, we need to be aware that many veterans and military retirees are seeking treatment outside of the VA in the civilian sector for various reasons.

Historically, distrust can be a major component of PTSD symptom exacerbation. A veteran may prefer to seek help outside of the military or governmental system. So, it is important for everyone concerned in these treatment fields, especially hypnotherapists, to be mindful of this information.

Now, let us return to the National Comorbidity Survey (1995). This was a sample of all U.S. citizens. This study wasn't just about combat veterans. If we examine the lifetime prevalence of post traumatic stress only among combat veterans, we find in that sample PTSD was very elevated. It was approximately 39%. This number is actually higher than the percentage reported by the National Vietnam Veterans Readjustment Study (Kulka, Schlenger, Fairbank, Hough, et al, 1990). It is also important to note that if a veteran has PTSD, then combat-related PTSD is much more probable to occur among men. These data are most likely a result of not having enough women represented in the sample. This does not mean that we should ignore the results. For men, combat-related PTSD has increased lifetime prevalence and a much greater likelihood of a delayed onset. This onset might sometimes occur decades later as a result of some trigger or life stressor. And, combat PTSD has a much greater chance of not responding to or being alleviated by treatment. Combat PTSD has a history of being very resistant to treatment. So **combat PTSD seems to be particularly harmful**.

Another study of Vietnam veterans, the National Vietnam Veterans' Readjustment Study (1990), from a representative sample of 3,000 combat veterans, non-combat era veterans, and civilians, the reported lifetime prevalence among males was 31%. Among females, the lifetime prevalence was 26%. Neither appears to be quite as elevated as the 39% of the National

Comorbidity Survey (1995), but both are still relatively high. The current prevalence among men is 15% and among women 8%. The prevalence among women is lower here, and yet in general, women have a higher prevalence of PTSD. This may be due to the exclusivity of the military sample. In Vietnam the females, many of whom were nurses, had more protective factors. They were older, had more advanced education, and were mostly officers. This does not compare well with a representative sample of all females. However, the recent data from the OIF and OEF groups indicate that women and men appear to have similar rates of PTSD. Remember, these are women who volunteered to be in the military and completed their training. This group is most likely very different from a national sample. So some of these gender differences are very interesting and there will be questions about them in the future as more data is recorded.

If we examine the prevalence of PTSD from other wars, for instance the Gulf War, the prevalence is only about 10% compared with approximately 30% in Vietnam. Currently, the Afghanistan and Iraq wars are really works in progress. The prevalence estimates for PTSD vary depending on what kind of criteria used. For instance, in Afghanistan they vary from 6% - 11.5% and in Iraq from approximately 12-20%. These are continually evolving statistics and honestly no one knows at this time exactly how the statistics will appear when these conflicts end. To compare this data with the Gulf War or the Vietnam War, statistics at this time would not give an accurate description of similarities or differences. So for now, we can speculate all we want but we must wait to see how everything will turn out.

This is what we do know now. These are the statistics concerning Operation Iraqi Freedom that we are aware of at the time of this writing. There were 4173 United States Military fatalities from 3/19/03 – 9/30/08. Of these, forty percent were resulting from Improved Explosive Device (IED) attacks. The majority of U.S. deaths were Army personnel at 2651. Of all fatalities, 31% resulted from hostile fire, 5% from helicopter crashes, and 15% friendly fire. The anger (victim of friendly fire) and guilt (perpetrator of friendly fire) can complicate PTSD symptoms quite a bit. Official reports indicate that U.S. Forces killed 1600 Iraqi civilians in August 2007 alone. According to the Congressional Research Service Report for Congress on Estimates of Civilian Casualties (2008), during the entire conflict thus far range from 34,832 to 793,663 depending on the source. When this book was begun in 2007, the number of daily attacks by insurgent forces averaged 160 a day.

Even though the numbers are still being recorded and we cannot make any statement as to how the statistics will evolve, it must be noted that OIF has the highest ratios PTSD when compared to any previous conflict right now. It is speculated that this is due to a constant threat condition. In Iraq, there is NO safe place and NO safe duty. Eighty-six percent of OIF troops personally know someone who has been killed during the conflict (Department of Defense, 2008). Over half of those serving in OIF (51%), have personally discovered dead bodies or decomposed human remains (DoD). Over three fourths (77%), have actively fired a weapon on the enemy and of those forty eight percent knew that they had killed enemy troops(DoD). Guilt is strongly related to complicated PTSD symptoms and a powerful motivator towards guilt is killing presumably innocent civilians. Therefore, it is very important to note that about twenty-eight percent of U.S. troops report that they have killed non-combatants(DoD).

In the history of PTSD it was mentioned that these symptoms were highly correlated with health issues among veterans. This is noted as far back as the American Civil War (Pizarro, Silver, & Prause, 2006). So, there is a further burden of PTSD. If a person suffers from PTSD, they are more likely to exhibit other problems both psychological and medical. They have an elevated risk of being diagnosed with other mental disorders. There are indications of increased additional anxiety disorders, major depression, or substance abuse disorders. Persons suffering from PTSD have a greater risk of suicide attempts, increased functional impairment, and reduced quality of life. In fact, if we examine the National Comorbidity Survey (1995) data, we may conclude that PTSD had the utmost influence of all anxiety disorders as an economic burden to our society.

Essentially, if one examines the odds ratio data from the National Comorbidity Survey (1995) for the risk of having an additional, different comorbid psychiatric disorder, such as depression, dysthymia, general anxiety disorder, or panic, etc., for those people with PTSD as compared to those without PTSD, they will find that if a person is male and has PTSD, they are almost six times more likley to have depression than if they don't have PTSD. And, if the person is female, the risk of having comorbid major depression is about 3.5 times larger. There are similar results concerning alcohol or drug abuse. If a person suffers from PTSD, they have a 2-3 times increased likelihood of having a comorbid substance abuse or dependence disorder than if you don't have PTSD. As a matter of fact, in every single case of anxiety and mood disorders, if a person is diagnosed with PTSD, they have a much greater probability of having a comorbid mental disorder diagnosis (Kessler, et al, 1995).

People who have PTSD symptoms are functionally impaired (Kessler, et al). The National Comorbidity Survey indicates that persons with PTSD have a 40% elevated risk of academic failure, a 30% elevated risk of teenage parenthood, a 60% elevated risk of marital problems, and 150% increased risk to be currently unemployed. All of these data indicate the possibility of impaired functioning and reduced quality of life. And, these statistics are for persons in general, not just veterans.

If we examine PTSD and functioning in veterans, we have two sources of information that are relevant, the National Comorbidity Survey (1995) and the National Vietnam Veterans' Readjustment Study (NVVRS) (1990). The data from these studies show agreement and reliability. Veterans with PTSD symptoms have an increase with problems holding a job. They also show higher rates of unemployment and being fired. They exhibit greater problems in their personal relationships. In terms of marriage, they show elevated rates of both divorce/separation and spouse abuse. It is indicated in these studies that they report generally poor health and increased limitations to physical functioning. And, they are often more likely to commit violent acts. So, it is very important to keep in mind that PTSD involves many other implications in terms of functional impairment.

The majority of persons who develop PTSD are known to recover from it. This will be important to keep in mind and explain to all clients during their client education in the first session. In so doing, we can create an expectation for recovery and success. But, according to the National Comorbidity Survey (1995), approximately 15-25% of people who developed symptoms of PTSD did not improve. PTSD is not a simple disorder. It is a disorder in which recovery is complicated. A lot of this data was obtained before there were treatments that worked. This means that many persons who did not recover during the time of these data might benefit strongly from current treatments. Many psychological and pharmacological treatments today show increased successes. Therefore, it will be interesting to see in the future how we might improve upon this. The question will be whether more people will recover from PTSD currently than have in the past because they will now receive more effective treatment. Hypnotic Exposure Therapy will most likely be a strong asset in improving the number of successes.

PTSD has a variable course and onset. Usually it appears within the first two years following the trauma, but onset may be delayed for quite some time. It may not manifest for many, many years. In the National Comorbidity Survey (1995), an episode of PTSD was likely to last about three years for people who got treatment and approximately five years for people who did not receive treatment. It is important to note that these data are based on reports of a single episode of PTSD. We must not forget that there is often the likely risk of having a PTSD relapse upon re-exposure to a traumatic event. The risk is highly elevated for this to occur. So, if we put these three and five year episodes in context, the client can have a sequence of 3 - 5 years of symptom episodes, based on the number of exposures and/or resulting relapse, depending on whether or not they have entered or completed treatment.

Symptom exacerbation appears very frequently in chronic or persistent PTSD cases. New traumas or stressful life events can trigger the reactivation of PTSD symptoms. Therefore, persons with PTSD are at an elevated risk for having a long period of suffering the symptoms. And like other chronic disorders, a series of relapses may occur along with periods of remission. When examining reactivation and exacerbation, we are looking for potential triggers. There are numerous stimuli that can reactivate PTSD symptoms among people who've experienced them before. A client may be exposed to reminders of the trauma, new traumatic events, a medical illness (particularly one that makes them feel helpless), bereavement, loss of a loved one, or any "normal" stressful life event that one could be involved in during the normal course of living. It appears that retirement may result in major issues. This may be one of the reasons why a lot of elder veterans who appeared to adjust reasonably well with their PTSD during the time they were working begin to exhibit PTSD symptoms later on in life. So remember these potential problems when assessing for PTSD. Once a client has suffered from PTSD symptoms, they are forever in jeopardy of having a relapse. This is very important to keep in mind concerning client care and educating our clients concerning their expectations. It is significant from the perspective of what potential situations they might expose themselves to and for some of the decisions they make in the future. Our goal is the education of our client to avoid or reduce the risk of entering a situation that could result in triggering a relapse of symptoms.

"The more we ignore the animals we are, the more likely it is that the fearful beast will be released"

– Sheldon Kopp

Chapter 4

Risk Factors for the Occurrence of PTSD

Let's examine the risk factors for Post Traumatic Stress Disorder. For any difficulty, when we talk about risk factors, we are talking about three distinct time periods. For PTSD, we use specific language: Pre-traumatic, peri-traumatic, and post-traumatic for each period. When we look at pre-traumatic risk factors, we want to know the factors that, prior to the trauma, might result in people being more likely to develop PTSD. When we investigate the peri-traumatic risks, we are asking what characteristics of the event in itself are risk factors. And finally, what might occur in the aftermath of the event (post-traumatic factors) that make it more likely for PTSD to emerge? Always keep in mind that correlational research is used to identify risks. Therefore, we cannot state that the risk factors of any type cause Post Traumatic Stress Disorder. However, if they are present, we are alerted to look closely at our clients for symptoms of PSTD because it may be likely.

First, there are many pre-traumatic risk factors to note. These correlates include adverse childhood experiences, female gender, an absence of practical social support, prior psychiatric issues or disorders, and coexisting stressful life events. There is also some speculation about genetic factors, particularly in relation to the serotonin transporter gene (Kilpatrick, D., Koenen, K., Ruggiero, K., Acierno, R., Galea, S., Resnick, H., et al., 2007). Although many pre-traumatic risk factors are found in epidemiological research, it appears that these are less significant than the peri-traumatic and the post-traumatic risk factors. Therefore, if a person experiences adverse childhood experiences or are female they might have a slightly increased risk of developing PSTD. However, as previously reported, the women are doing just as well as the men in OIF and OEF according to current data. So, there are more significant risk factors that will have a stronger influence on whether or not someone develops PTSD symptoms. Those are the peri-traumatic and the post-traumatic correlates.

When we examine peri-traumatic risk factors, all PTSD research, not just in war zones but with accidents, child abuse, and disaster research, we discover a dose response curve. The greater the severity of the traumatic experience, the more likely the person will suffer from PTSD symptoms. Therefore, the degree to which a person experiences the stressor can be a major predictor. This is shown to be a stronger predictor of PTSD than the pre-traumatic risk factors. So, a person who experiences as increased perception of their life being endangered or the more a loved one is in danger, the greater fear or risk they will experience.

And, the greater the feeling of fear, helplessness, and horror a person experiences, the increased likelihood a person will develop PTSD. Animal studies, which can be an effective means of doing research on PTSD, have tried to create simulated traumatic stressors in the laboratory that are both unpredictable and uncontrollable. The resulting consensus is that experience of an increased perception of life or loved one's life being endangered is a measurable risk factor (Kulka, Schlenger, Fairbank, Hough, et al, 1990). The greater the feelings of helplessness, that is, the expectation of more danger to come with an inability to know when it might occur and the feeling that there is nothing one can do about it, is a strong risk factor. These are the peri-traumatic risk factors that appear to predict the consequent severity of PTSD symptoms.

The final set of risk factors, that is the post-traumatic, seem to be the most significant. Among those, one of the strongest is the amount of social support following the event. Brewin (2005) completed an analysis of all known

research; including pre-traumatic, peri-traumatic, and post-traumatic factors for risks. He found that if a person who experienced trauma had social support, the likelihood of developing PTSD was going to be vastly reduced. And, you might recall, the traditional Vietnam War veteran, had little or no social support. They were stigmatized. Some were even picketed, protested, and railed against. If it was our cultural intention, we probably could not have created a worse case scenario for an environment in which post-traumatic stress could occur.

The current climate in the country, given the Iraq and Afghanistan wars, appears to be in direct contrast to Vietnam. Whatever a person's political opinions about the appropriateness of the war, the support for the troops and veterans is most likely unanimous. This is a very positive environmental factor when considering the risk for PTSD to develop and the difficulties with treatment. Also, there are studies demonstrating that social support can even counteract genetic susceptibility (Kilpatrick, D., Koenen, K., Ruggiero, K., Acierno, R., Galea, S., Resnick, H., et al., 2007). As therapists, and as members of this post-traumatic scene, we are also part of this post-traumatic social network. So, the sooner we meet and treat people, the more likely it is that we can prevent the development of more serious PTSD symptoms.

Another problem is very important when considering OIF veterans in particular. Given the character of PTSD, if the veteran has been continually exposed to experiences that are stressful or traumatic with no safe place or safe duty, then that's a post-traumatic aspect that's going to increase the likelihood of PTSD. The Iraqi conflict in particular is a violent and unpredictable situation, where one is continually in the situation and the anxiety is never going to stop for an extended period of time. How does a therapist in a war zone permit people in treatment to still remain in a stressful situation and hope to be effective? That's also true in abusive situations as well as war zones. It's also true in prisoner of war situations or concentration camps. Ongoing stresses and experiences of traumatic cues in particular are powerful risk factors for PTSD.

"It is a great mistake in practice to treat an archetype as if it were a mere name, word, or concept. It is far more than that: it is a piece of life, an image connected with the living individual by the bridge of emotion"

– C.G Jung

Chapter 5

Transpersonal Risk Approaches to PTSD

In transpersonal psychology, the Gods and Goddesses of War, appearing in many cultures under many other guises, have a strong influence in the evolution of societies. As mentioned earlier, "war" has appeared to humans by many names for a very long time. As previously observed, when we examine some classic myths described by authors and poets from the past, we may observe that evidence of PTSD is present in a transpersonal, archetypal form. The mythological significance of this disorder presented in the warrior archetypes of Achilles and Odysseus in the Greek tragedies by Homer, *The Iliad* and *The Odyssey*, are of great importance when approaching the disorder from a transpersonal perspective (Nagy, 1979).

In the story of *The Iliad*, we find the effects of Post Traumatic Stress described in the behavior of Achilles. His anger at the prize of victory being taken from him is described. We are told of his threat of leaving the battle forever to turn his back on the war. This feeling of betrayal might exist in Operation Iraqi Freedom or Operation Enduring Freedom, when troops find that the reasons for being in Iraq were based on misinformation or that the mission in Afghanistan was never completed prior to moving the focus to Iraq and thus resulting in increased difficulties that will need to be addressed soon. Early in the OIF conflict, the military equipment was found to be inferior and did not offer the troops proper protection. The troops' weapons and gear are essential to their success. Their very survival depends on proper functioning equipment. The troops in both countries found they had inappropriate body armor or unacceptably armored vehicles. Statements by our leaders might have given the impression that they did not care. The military itself gives a sense of moral rightness to behaviors that lead to death and destruction. The modern warrior is often at the mercy of his or her superiors when it comes to supplies. Poor equipment equals death. The idea of betrayal by one's officers or political leaders tends to destroy the moral fabric upon which the military service is grounded. The idea that photo op "Mission Accomplished" celebrations could occur while the troops were still fighting and dying with no end in sight surely must create these feelings. According to Shay (1994), this greatly increases the risks of PTSD. We must be aware of these feelings if they arise in our clients and not judge their beliefs.

There are several ways that these feelings may be complicated. Assignment of blame may be to the self. The veterans may search themselves to try to examine what they could have done differently. They may place blame on some officer or politician. Their anger may be directed at God. As one veteran stated to me, "If there is a God and he allows these things to happen, I don't want anything to do with him". That may be the ultimate feeling of betrayal.

Shay (2002) also considers the story of *The Odyssey* and the effects of returning home on the combat, hardened veteran. In this story, our veteran Odysseus finds himself interacting with those "soft" civilians who have not had the experience of being in a battle where death is hovering continuously. He is angered at those mere mortals who sat safely in their comfortable life. He knows how easy it is to die or kill in that other world. It seems that he lost himself in the war that appears to remain with him as part of the psyche. He discovers that the battles he thought he left behind remain. He finds the memory of them is now a constant companion in his anxiety.

The skills a warrior learns to be successful are not conducive to civilian success and reintegration. From a transpersonal approach, he has lost both his "old" self and any sense of meaning. He has returned to society in combat mode. His skills include control of emotions, deception (lies & cunning), ability to respond instantly with deadly force, vigilance (or paranoia), strength, quickness, stealth, skill at acquiring supplies/weapons by any means necessary, adaptation to cruel conditions, and use of multiple lethal skills/weapons. For what civilian occupation does this prepare one?

Our veterans have trained themselves to avoid pain, both physical and psychological. The pain of wounds, grief, or fear might be deadly in combat. Some may return needing an adrenaline fix. They may find themselves seeking excitement in dangerous activities. Veterans may treat work like a combat mission. They may feel that no one else can do it. They might turn life into a work addiction by working more than 40 hour weeks, not for the money but for the mission. There may be no safe place. As mentioned earlier, Iraq was unique for some time in that there was no where to relax or feel safe from attack. This could manifest at home in the form of constant vigilance or paranoia. The veteran may feel this is necessary for survival. Male veterans might consider females dangerous or untrustworthy. They may be used for sex but not intimacy or sharing of feelings.

Our veterans may experience guilt. They may be haunted by the "ghosts" of those who died. Their friends may have died yet they survived. Some may feel that dying would have been easier. Finally, many struggle with finding meaning by attempting to discover the truth behind the conflict. They might question, "Why did we really go there to fight and die?" This is a question that often has no answer. This may be especially problematic with OIF, where the reasons changed as politicians attempted to justify their actions.

The troops most likely left for war with a transpersonal view of justice, right, wrong, and fighting for a higher purpose. The loss of this view can complicate the symptoms of PTSD. Vietnam veterans may have felt they had to hide their involvement in an unpopular war. Social support was not there for them to assist in their re-integration into society. The OIF veteran must deal with mixed support. There are still debates as to whether we should have even invaded in the first place. Without unified support, their returns may be very difficult also. Veterans cannot help being aware of the gulf between their personal warrior myths and the myth of the predominant culture at home. Many rationalize this away by saying warriors know the risks they are taking when they sign on for the job. However, these are often young, impressionable men and women whose dedication to honor, duty, and country may have been exposed to the harsh facts of war that cause them deep distress and dissonance. Many returning veterans firmly believe their actions result from duty and try not to reflect on their war involvement in other ways. In moments of reflection, veterans may find themselves with no personal, positive meaningful story or narrative concerning the conflict to justify their involvement.

The initial treatment of PTSD hypnotically will not restore meaning or purpose to life. Our clients must be relatively free of their symptoms in order for this to occur. They must create a narrative. The story of their life must be written fully. Only then can meaning return. Therefore, it is best to continue with the complete description of hypnotic treatment. We will finish by returning to myth and meaning from a transpersonal perspective in discussion of our last client sessions.

"The significant problems we face cannot be solved at the same level of thinking we were at when we created them"

– Albert Einstein

Chapter 6

Cognitive Implications: Change Your Thinking and Transform Your Life

We are the way we are because of the thoughts we think. Until we change the way we think, then nothing else will change. A major concern of trauma treatment is the integration of thoughts concerning the event. The idea here is that trauma is represented differently in memory than other events. These memories have pathological features, for if they are activated, they result in stress reactions or avoidance. Hypnotherapy has long been utilized to assist in the transformation of thoughts toward more positive outcomes. Therefore, hypnotic therapy is a good fit in working to integrate more healthy cognitions about a traumatic event.

One theory of thought processes (cognitions) involved in PTSD is called emotion processing theory (Foa & Rothbaum, 1998). The theory centers on memory encoding. PTSD cognitions result from impaired emotional processing of the trauma due to the encoding of a memory that has distinctiveness in several ways that make it hard to modify. Foa & Rothbaum (1998) called this a pathological fear construction in memory. This fear structure is composed of aspects of memory that relate to what occurred, the stimuli that were at hand during the trauma, the person's own responses during the trauma, and his or her understandings of what happened. These PTSD-related memories are believed to be very easily activated and intensely disruptive. They are not organized the way that memories for non-traumatic experiences seem to be. They may contain several unrealistic elements where harmless stimuli or circumstances are connected with flight or avoidance responses that the person may have utilized at the time of the trauma. And, they often include a number of flawed assessments or interpretations. To summarize the theory of PTSD as impaired emotional processing of trauma:

There is a large pathological fear construction of traumatic event:

- It contains trauma stimuli, responses, and meaning elements
- It is easily activated (ambiguous stimuli) and disruptively intense
- It may be disorganized and fragmented
- There may be unrealistic elements
- Harmless stimuli are associated with escape or avoidance responses
- These thought structures contain erroneous evaluations or interpretations, i.e.:
  - "Anxiety will persist until escape"
  - "Fear will cause harm" (go crazy, become ill)
  - "These consequences are terrible"

The theory of emotional processing focuses attention on

some areas of interest to us. The first is that it is appropriate for treatment success to activate the fear construction. The idea is to activate the fear memory so that we might help the client to transform it. If not, it may remain in a structure that is not open to change. Hypnosis provides an effective altered state for dealing with dissociative imagery anamnesis (Williams & Sommer, 2002). Therefore, hypnotic exposure therapy is partially aimed at simply activating the fear memory. We know we have activated this area when we observe emotional arousal taking place here and now in the therapeutic situation. Remember, we want to activate the fear structure. At the same time, we may assist the client to integrate new data that contradicts the dysfunctional elements of the fear structure and helps to correct the problem. This may simply result in the person now finding the ability to relax and feel more physical comfort in the face of the frightening memory. It could be something that the therapist relates during the experience. It may even be that the client discovers through the therapist's behavior how other people might react with support rather than rejection. This new information needs to be made available because the fearful memories are nearly always triggered in the hypnotic session, but that doesn't result in healing. These memories are unpredictable and tremendously upsetting. If they are just turned off by some kind of escape or avoidance, this just reinforces the difficulty.

Therefore, there is nothing changing and no new therapeutic information is being integrated to change that memory into a useful form. Emotion processing directs attention to the way that the narrative or story of trauma changes. Using hypnotic exposure therapy, the client can integrate the images/emotions into a verbal narrative, begin to distance from or change the story, and begin to remove associated anxiety (Foa, Keane, & Friedman, 2000). Hopefully, it changes into a form that becomes empowering as a person goes through it repeatedly in the hypnotic exposure process. This leads to traumatic strength as opposed to traumatic stress. The result can be a better organization of memory. The story may increase in complexity with fewer unfinished thoughts and repetitions. This will be addressed in detail when we discuss the transpersonal aspects of the therapy. The basic elements involved in the emotional processing aspects of hypnotic exposure therapy are listed below:

- Through exposure the fear cognitions must be activated in order to be changed
- New curative information must be provided that is incompatible with pathological elements of fear cognitions
- The story changes in successive retellings
    - Fewer unfinished thoughts, repetitions
    - Increased complexity of narrative

Brewin and Holmes (2003) differentiate between two kinds of recollections that are encoded in traumatic experiences. Some recollections are verbally accessible and some are accessible by situation or environment. This is considered the Dual Representation Theory of trauma cognitions (Brewin and Holmes). Verbally accessible memories (VAM) are the types of things that clients can say to us about trauma if we ask them. We simply ask, "What happened to you?" Then, the client gives us a description of things that happened. These recollections are depictions of their conscious knowledge of the trauma. The client can deliberately recall these memories when asked about the trauma. And within these memories we might discover the narrative meanings we are attempting to help clients discover. They might say something such as, "I don't know why I didn't act. I froze. I was a coward in the situation." The judgments that the client makes are usually verbally accessible memories. But, there are also memories of trauma that cannot be consciously accessed. These are situationally accessible memories (SAM). The memories that are accessed automatically when the person is in a situation reminiscent of the presence of trauma cues or reminders (Brewin & Holmes).

The psychological theory of classical conditioning is related to this process. For instance, a veteran is walking down the street and sees someone that resembles "the enemy", or may observe a motor vehicle that looks similar to a car that was present when a bomb was detonated. This may result in a series of internal, physiological and emotional reactions that are automatic reactions to these situational cues. However, the client might not be able to remember that experience or describe that car when asked to consciously recall what happened in the trauma event. Therefore, the situation cued memories are the ones that are connected to powerful, classically conditioned emotional responses. From a cognitive view, it is useful to make a distinction between those two types of memory. And so, we need to be aware that:

- Trauma often leads to two types of memory
  - Verbally-accessible memories (VAM)
    - Recall of the conscious experience of the trauma

    - Can be deliberately retrieved
    - Especially, "meanings"
- Situational-accessible memories (SAM)
    - Cannot be consciously accessed
    - Memories accessed automatically when in presence of trauma cues/reminders
    - Conditioned emotional reactions

In Dual Representation Theory (Brewin & Holmes, 2003), there may be three different kinds of conclusions reached after working through the trauma or emotional processing of the trauma. First, the best outcome would be completion and integration, in which a client imagines the trauma, revisits it, engages in a process of re-experience in trauma emotions, perhaps so that habituation may take place. This would be the positive working through of the experience that may occur with hypnotic exposure therapy. Second, some individuals, however, might get stuck in a kind of never-ending emotional processing. This can be a type of rumination process where the client thinks over and over again about the characteristics of what happened. This may result in a constant preoccupation with the results of the trauma without any problem solving or resolution to the difficulties. Finally, clients may use inhibition of processing by increasing behavior that requires their concentration. For example, they might become a workaholic. As they are requiring themselves to concentrate on other things, they may find a reduction in symptoms and some improvement in their ability to function. However, they are actually continuing to pursue their fearful avoidance of trauma triggers. In this case, they may experience somatic symptoms, that is, physical symptoms without any discernable physical cause. And they may become more vulnerable to the thoughts becoming reactivated later in life, such as, when veterans who have been a workaholics for many years retire and discover the thoughts they believed to be eliminated begin to return while becoming even more intrusive and prominent. To review, there are three possible conclusions for emotional processing (Brewin & Holmes):

- Completion/integration
- Unrelieved emotional processing (Rumination)
    - Enduring preoccupation with end results of trauma and intrusive memories
- Premature inhibition of processing
    - Active avoidance
    - Continued phobic avoidance
    - Somatic complaints
    - Vulnerable to reactivation later in life

Dual Representation Theory directs our attention to focus on what are called the "hotspots of a memory", also known as the situationally accessible memories (Brewin & Holmes, 2003). We want to identify what types of situations trigger those memories and what happens with a person as a result of exposure. The client is invited to talk about the memories and transform memories triggered by situation into verbal memories by putting the experience into words and conscious awareness. As a result, we hope that the client may change the representation of the memory. That is the essence of what happens in hypnotic exposure therapy. A person is triggered by those reminders, remembers what happens, and, while in a relaxed state they are encouraged to keep talking about the trauma. The theory is that these verbally accessible memories will be easier to manage for the client. Therefore, when the client experiences a trigger in the future, he or she will be more able to use appropriate coping skills because the trigger will elicit the verbally accessible memory rather that just the situation cued, conditioned emotional response. In sessions, these SAMS (hot spots) should be identified and during hypnotic exposure, transformed into VAMS. As a result, these new VAMS will compete with the SAMS when triggers are encountered.

Ehlers and Clark's (2000) cognitive theory of PTSD makes some related points while directing us to some additional features. Ehlers and Clark indicate that there are two critical memory processes that result in a sense of persistent threat after trauma. This sense of constant threat is to blame for sustaining acute stress responses and moving them towards the resulting unremitting Post Traumatic Stress Disorder. These essential thoughts related to ongoing threat result from the way the memory is encoded, the character of the memory, and how it may be linked to other memories (Ehlers & Clark). This seems comparable to what Foa describes as the pathological fear memory (1998). Ehlers and Clark take this a step farther by talking about the evaluation of trauma and its following pathology. Therefore, the clients' personal assessment of the trauma in terms of intrapersonal thoughts about their symptoms, reactions, and experience is of great importance. Those self evaluations they make, such as, judgments of personal weakness, guilt, and distrust in others, play a role in maintaining a sense of chronic threat. Finally, Ehlers and Clark's cognitive theory emphasizes the behavioral responses, cognitive responses, and avoidance reactions already discussed that can prevent cognitive change and habituation from occurring. As a result, the disorder is maintained indefinitely. To review Ehlers and Clark's (2000) cognitive theory of PTSD:

- Two critical processes lead to sense of ongoing threat after trauma
  - Differences in encoding of memory and links to other memories
  - Differences in trauma evaluation and it's following pathology (e.g., symptoms)

The cognitive theory of PTSD directs our attention to the nature of trauma memories. The theory is that trauma memories are encoded primarily as sensory impressions. There is an impression with these memories that they are happening right now in the moment, are very severe, and are not to be found in the past. In fact, many of the original sensory impressions and emotions that were experienced in the traumatic situation itself seem to be felt in the memory as if happening now. And, they are being unwillingly triggered by a wide range of stimuli and situations. This appears to be the same theory discussed as memories accessed by exposure to certain situations and conditioned emotional responses. Often, these intense emotions and physical sensations are automatically triggered. Therefore, clients will find themselves experiencing the emotional affect while they might have no memory of the trauma. They may not even be able to connect their emotional or physical responses with the trauma event. People with PTSD have personal negative evaluations of the traumatic event and/or the resulting responses that have the frequent effect of producing an illusion of serious current threat. Therefore, they often experience continued anxiety and stress, even without the presence of the situational stressors. This continual, chronic perceived threat also motivates behavioral and cognitive reactions that prevent cognitive change and therefore maintain the disorder.

Ehlers and Clark (2000) focus on the personal negative evaluations of the events and resulting pathological responses that relate to a continuing sense of threat. For example, if clients decide that they cannot protect themselves, the world is too dangerous, or people cannot be trusted, then those cognitive appraisals of the world would indicate that the world is going to continue to be dangerous. How can the world not be dangerous for the person who can't protect themselves? The client is predicting the future and the prediction is that bad things will happen. Therefore, the clients' negative cognitions sustain fears of ongoing threats. If nothing changes these thoughts, they maintain the traumatic stress reactions. These negative cognitions or memories are characterized by:

- Mainly sensory impressions and not verbal
- The sense that they are "happening right now"
- The re-experience of original emotions and sensory impressions
- Emotional responses without recollection
- Involuntary re-experiencing triggered by many stimuli and situations

Let's look at the hypnotic treatment implications of this cognitive model. First, the client needs detailed recall of the trauma memory. Then, it may be integrated into the context of the individual's life experience both before and after the trauma event. The theory is that often the client may have a very brief and sensory traumatic memory. For example, the person might remember an explosion. But the memory does not include any other following information. It may be that the person assisted others with injuries or escaped harm while others died. There is no resolution or ending. Facts about returning to safety are missing. The traumatic memory just related to damage, death, or destruction. So, it may be useful to organize the story of the event to contain many elements of traumatic memory. Also, Ehlers and Clark (2000) indicate that we need to identify the problem evaluations or appraisals that sustain this sense of threat and assist the client to confront them. Finally, as with most cognitive behavioral treatment methods, it is recommended that we should intervene and begin to eliminate dysfunctional coping strategies that prevent recovery, like substance abuse or extreme avoidance. To summarize Ehlers and Clark:

- Trauma memory is elaborated and integrated into context of individual's before and after experience
- Problematic appraisals that sustain feelings of threat are modified
- Dysfunctional coping strategies that thwart improvement need to be eliminated

Exposure and clear recall are key elements to treatment that are embedded in many of the best cognitive behavioral evidence based treatments Therefore, these cognitive behavioral models

lead us inevitably to the use of hypnotic exposure therapy.

"In dealing with fear, the only way out is in."

– Sheldon Kopp

Chapter 7

Hypnotic Exposure Treatment for PTSD in Theory and Practice:

Hypnosis is considered an effective treatment for PTSD and there is evidence that it may facilitate, intensify, and shorten treatment (Cardena et al., 2000). PTSD treatment involving hypnosis is divided into four stages: Ego Strengthening (Safety & Stabilization), Accessing and Mastering of Emerging Traumatic Material (Accessing Traumatic Material), Re-association (Resolving Traumatic Experience), and Integration & New Identity (Phillips & Frederick, 1995). Watkins (1949) used hypnosis extensively in the treatment of "war neurosis" with much success.

The following conditions should be met when considering hypnotic exposure therapy (Williams & Sommer, 2002):

1) Clients must be able to form images related to the trauma

2) They must be capable of following instructions from the therapists related to forming these images

3) They must be capable of handling intense arousal and increase in symptoms (beginning treatment)

4) They must be in relatively good health (for example: no heart condition, etc.)

5) They must have a stable home environment or strong social support

6) They should not be abusing alcohol or drugs

Evidence suggests that immediate debriefing following a traumatic event does more harm than good (McNally, 2003). Therefore, hypnotic exposure treatment should only be used when the client has met the diagnostic criteria for Post Traumatic Stress Disorder and not merely been exposed to a traumatic event or simply suffering from Acute Stress Disorder.

The research has not established the selection criteria needed to determine whether or not to use hypnotic exposure therapy. In the end, this will require the therapist's clinical judgment. The basic five items previously listed make for a good start. However, a number of issues will need to be considered. Certainly, we need to get a physician's approval stating that the client is an appropriate candidate for a stressful therapy. It is obvious that the veteran whose health may not be very good is most likely not an appropriate client for this method. So, someone with a high risk coronary artery disease or severe heart condition might be a poor candidate for exposure therapy. If there is evidence of a previous substance abuse/dependence disorder, we want to make sure that our clients are in established remission. If not, we need to take measures to put together supports or counseling for them with their substance abuse. We want to verify that their home environment is stable. If they're homeless, living on the street, going through a divorce, or in an abusive home environment, clearly we're not going to do this type of therapy. It may be that now is just not the right time. We want to be sure of their emotional stability. The stressful nature of exposure therapy may be too much and create an unstable mental health episode.

Veterans with personality disorder traits, particularly antisocial or borderline traits, are often not amenable to reintegration through hypnotic therapies (Brende, 1984). Antisocial personality traits involve a pervasive pattern of behavior where the rights of others are disregarded or violated. This disorder is considered to be in evidence when a minimum of three of the following traits are exhibited: a) repeated performance of acts that are grounds for arrest, b) repeated deceit or lying, c) failure to plan ahead or impulsive behaviors, d) repeated physical fights or assaults, e) reckless disregard for the safety of self or others, f) repeated irresponsible behavior, such as failure to maintain work or honor financial obligations, or g) lack of remorse for harmful behavior to others.

Borderline personality traits involve a pervasive pattern of behavior demonstrating unstable interpersonal relationships, self image, and emotions, along with extremely impulsive behaviors. The disorder is considered to be exhibited with a minimum of five of the following traits: a) frantic efforts to avoid real or imagined abandonment, b) unstable and intense interpersonal relationships where the other is characterized by extremes of idealization and devaluation, c) unstable self image or sense of self, d) impulsivity in behaviors that become self-damaging (at least two of the following, i.e. sex, spending, substance abuse, reckless driving, or binge eating), d) recurring suicidal or self mutilating behavior, e) marked reactivity and instability of mood, f) chronic feelings of emptiness, g) inappropriate, intense anger, or h) transient, stress related paranoia or dissociation.

Any client demonstrating these traits will not be a good

candidate for hypnotic exposure therapy. However, it should be noted here that some veterans of OIF and OEF, upon returning home, are being diagnosed with personality disorders that are always considered "pre-existing (lifelong) conditions" and then are denied services from the VA (House Veteran's Affairs Committee Report, 2008). In the past six years, over 22,500 military personnel have been discharged due to personality disorders (HVACR). Veterans diagnosed with personality disorders can seek disability benefits, but again they must show that their condition was aggravated by military service. This can be a difficult process. A person who has also experienced childhood or multiple traumas may develop a more complex form of PTSD, which involves identification with a "victim" mythology where fear and safety dominate their lives (Williams & Sommer, 2002).

Also, a poorly timed hypnotic intervention may be ineffective and increase resistance to treatment or disintegrative regression. Avoid clients who appear too omnipotent or have unstable ego boundaries (Brende). It may be that hypnotically repeating the situation again and again as called for in an exposure process might have the effect of intensifying the anger, shame, guilt, self-accusation, feelings of failure, and "What if?" thoughts connected with performance in the traumatic conditions rather than improve symptoms (Pitman et al., 1991).

Most importantly, we want to know if our clients are motivated to change. For this type of treatment, we need highly motivated individuals. If not, they may decide to leave treatment early on and not have the time to reduce their distress. This may leave them at a lower level of functioning than before the treatment. We want to discuss this exposure treatment with a client in significant detail, educate them about it, and then make a well informed and reasonable decision. If any client has had a history of involvement in many treatment programs, it may be useful to examine previous records or contact prior therapists to find how well the client has previously engaged in treatment or how well he or she had participated in treatment. This form of therapy is hard work with intense and emotionally difficult involvement. Therefore, it might be best used with clients, who have been well-informed about their problems while showing a dedication to improvement, possibly by demonstrating regular attendance and willingness to participate. To recap the selection criteria concerns involving clinical judgment include:

- Verify medical status (get medical release from physician)
- Establish substance abuse status
- Screen for environmental stability
- Screen emotional stability and coping skills
    - Suicide ideation
    - Psychosis
- Determine the motivation level of client
- Verify social support, cooperation, and problems

All treatment begins with a detailed assessment to determine if PTSD is actually present and if there are other clinical problems which might respond to hypnotherapy. Hypnotherapy is considered an effective method to assist, strengthen, and condense treatment for PTSD (Cardena et al., 2000). The therapeutic term used most often today is imaginal exposure therapy (Foa & Rothbaum, 1998). However, not all imaginal exposure therapy will use techniques that are considered to be hypnosis. Again, hypnotic treatment of PTSD involves four stages: ego strengthening, accessing traumatic material, resolving traumatic experience, and integration/creating meaning (Phillips & Frederick, 1995). Hypnotic Exposure is indicated as a treatment in all cases where the client exhibits the criteria for diagnosable PTSD. The client may also have PTSD and related problems such as anger, anxiety, depression, guilt, shame, relationship issues, and some alcohol or drug use. Once more, when considering Hypnotic Exposure therapy, the following conditions should be met: Clients must be capable of forming images related to the trauma, following instructions from the therapists related to forming these images, handling intense arousal and increase in symptoms, in relatively good health, have a stable home environment or strong social support, and not be abusing alcohol or drugs (Williams & Sommer, 2002). The alcohol and drug abuse is best evaluated by a professional who has specific training in this area before moving ahead. It is not always necessary that clients be sober as their sobriety may increase as a direct result of learning more appropriate ways of dealing with their PTSD.

Also, based on research by Foa, Hembree, and Rothbaum (2007), one must **not use** Hypnotic Exposure Therapy if a client:

- Is currently threatening suicide or homicide
- Has a recorded history of self injury or self mutilation that is currently active
- Exhibits psychosis, is out of touch with reality or actively

hallucinating.

- Is currently in an abusive relationship (either victim or perpetrator)
- As a result of treatment might increase their exposure to danger (too relaxed to be safe as in a war zone)
- Is alcohol or drug dependent (possibly as a result of self medicating PTSD symptoms?)
- Has no clear memory of any trauma (memory recovery must be attempted first).

These issues must be dealt with separately and prior to any type of exposure to traumatic memories. The health and safety of the client, therapist, and others may well be at stake here. If a prospective client meets these qualifying criteria, it is appropriate to move ahead with therapy.

Often, it is helpful to explain the characteristics of the PTSD diagnosis to clients so they might better understand their conditions. This is best accomplished by simply describing or listing the criteria to the client in a conversational manner and gauging their reactions/responses. For instance:

- PTSD is an anxiety disorder that may develop after an event is witnessed or experienced that involves an actual or perceived threat to life and limb.
- Your emotional reaction to this experience resulted in feelings of intense helplessness, horror, or terror.
- You may re-experience this event, sort of like being there again in your mind or having "flashbacks". Or, you may

relive the event in nightmares

- You might avoid anything that might remind you directly or cue a reminder of the experience.
- You might have symptoms we call increased arousal, making it hard to sleep or concentrate, increasing your vigilance of your surroundings for threats, making you jump or startle easily, or resulting in poor ability to focus or concentrate.

As rapport between the therapist and the client develops, the therapist should make every effort to determine the client's specific needs. Areas of specific interest may include:

- The client's view of the problem
- Treatment goals that focus on those needs in appropriate ways, according to the therapist's contribution
- Treatment goals that result from the client's views, judgments, and preferences
- Current problems and factors that led to their development
- Factors that maintain problems
- Formulation of client needs based on responses from client and therapist
- Building treatment goals around needs
- Sometimes, a treatment contract is best negotiated out of the assessment procedure. Therefore, negotiation of a treatment contract, along with goals and processes, might best be accomplished now.

Assessment itself is based on information from an assortment of resources. As therapists we must be aware that our patient's verbal self report of what he or she is doing in the social environment is not always the most accurate or useful account for making treatment decisions. Our clients frequently do not identify the triggers or influences on their behavior. They might describe these influences in ways that would be different from those of an outside observer. Therefore, always attempt to complement the assessment information received from discussion with the patient by talking with significant others and gaining input on their perceptions of the situation. Observe the behavior of the client in session. If possible, it might be helpful to observe the client in his or her natural environment or in interactions with other people outside of the office. There are helpful questionnaires available to assist us in gathering information systematically but they are not always needed. Also, our clients should be encouraged to self monitor their own behavior by completing journals or diary handouts for us that help to focus attention on the goals of treatment. Any self monitoring information can be important in the assessment procedure. To summarize, the following areas can be of great importance during individual client assessment:

- Talking with the client
- Conversation with significant others
- Observing the client in session
- Observing the client in his or her natural environment
- Questionnaires
- Self-monitoring data

Assessment efforts from a cognitive focus will be very specific about the triggers for emotional upset and what stimuli in the client's environment actually seem to set off the problem feelings or actions that are causing them difficulty. It is helpful to identify those very specifically as we may need this information for more directive hypnotherapy. This helps us to understand the thoughts that lead to problem behaviors of our clients and gives us a basis for hypnotic direction to respond in a different way when exposed to those triggers. We are looking for these thoughts so that we might assist the client to change them. "Change your thoughts and change your life", so to speak. We need to be clear on what our clients are thinking. We need to understand what they are experiencing and have them explain their responses in significant detail. We need to know what they are thinking, doing, feeling, and experiencing in response to environmental triggers. We want to know what their thoughts to themselves are in the situation, what concrete behavior they are actually engaged in, and what they are feeling in their body or physiology. Finally, we must assess what happens after the client's behavioral reactions. If a client is avoiding a trauma cue, then what happens? What happens to their thoughts, symptoms, and emotions? How do other people respond to their reactions? Frequently, other people's responses can have a resulting influence on the client's behavior. Are they rewarding productive coping skills? Are they rewarding maladaptive behavior? How do these rewards influence the client? All of these issues will be very important if we decide to use hypnosis in ways beyond exposure therapy to modify cognitions. In summary, during our client assessment we need to identify:

- "Triggers"

  – The stimuli that set off the problem thoughts, emotions, and behaviors.

- Reactions and responses
  - What precisely does the person think, feel, do, and experience?

- Recognition of consequences
  - What happens after?
  - What are other people's reactions to the client's responses?

One area of the assessment we have not discussed is brain damage and trauma. As mentioned earlier in the history of PTSD, a neurological explanation from WWI for these injuries was called "Shell-shock". It was theorized that being exposed to artillery blasts of big cannons somehow damaged the neural connections in the brain. In the current wars in Iraq and Afghanistan we do appear to have a genuine shell-shock. It is called traumatic brain injury. Many people who have traumatic brain injury also have PTSD. Traumatic "flash backs" involve the same area of the brain that is activated in epileptic seizures, that is, the hippocampus. Prolonged stress has measurable effects on both body and mind. To think that the brain is somehow separate from the body or there is a mind/body dichotomy, particularly from a transpersonal view, is a disservice to our clients. PTSD is related to a series of physical illnesses, such as heart disease, asthma, diabetes, ulcers, and possibly cancer (Bremner, 2002). We must be sure that our client's medical release does not indicate brain damage that may interfere or prevent successful hypnotic exposure treatment.

Often, stress alone appears to have detrimental effects on cognition, memory, and learning. Specifically, the hippocampus is affected with deficits in memory and the ability to learn new information. Stress leads to elevated cortisol. These high levels of the hormone may cause physical brain damage and can also lead to feelings of depression and fatigue. Cortisol is a major contributor to aging, disease, poor memory. The amygdale is also involved in negative emotional processing and some persons who have been exposed to trauma show lesions on the amygdala and increased fear/startle responses (Bremner, 2002). Hypnotic relaxation techniques can aid in reducing the stress response and output of cortisol. Another benefit of hypnosis can be the relaxed body's ability to enhance physical healing and repair. It is important that an appropriate physical exam occurs before continuing further with treatment.

From the assessment and relationship building process, we begin trauma education. It is very important that the client understands his or her experience. This is the foundation of client education. We are going to ask a lot of our clients in hypnotic exposure treatment because they have much to do and experience. We need to be sure that they are given the appropriate information with which to develop a strong rational and understanding regarding everything we ask them to do. They will most likely want to proceed when what we ask them to do seems to be appropriate to them. The educational process must help them to understand in significant detail how trauma affects them. It needs to help them clarify what the impacts of traumatic stress are on individuals in general and on themselves. What is post traumatic stress disorder? What does recovery entail? What will most likely happen in treatment, what do they need to do, how is it that improvement will manifest? The goal is to have an educated, active, and motivated client. Trauma education is essential to that objective. Again, some topics that need to be addressed during client education are:

- In what ways does trauma generally affect an individual?
- What is PTSD?
- What will happen during treatment?
- What is involved in recovery?
- What is the strong justification for treatment?

To begin our clients' education about therapy, it may be best to answer the question, "What is hypnotic exposure therapy?" The short answer is that hypnotic exposure therapy is a way to emotionally process the traumatic experience in a way to reduce PTSD symptoms, integrate the experience, and give it meaning that is helpful in achieving growth. It may be similar to the rationale used in horseback riding when one is thrown from a horse. It is best to get back on and ride out the fear until it is no longer a problem. I can relate a personal experience along those lines. One dark night I hit a German Shepherd on my motorcycle at 55 miles per hour and suffered a crash. For over a month following, I had nightmares of the crash over and over, waking up in a sweat with my heart racing. When the motorcycle was repaired (and my body), I was afraid of riding in the country or at night because I could not see far enough ahead. The anxiety was intense. So, I took short excursions, after reaching a relaxed state, into those places and times that caused my distress until it dissipated. Now, I know that the traumas that are experienced in war are far beyond falling from a horse or wrecking a motorcycle, but the idea is the same. The hypnotic exposure is the "ride" that leads to decreased distress and a return to a more normal existence.

The basic elements of the hypnotic exposure program are as follows:

- Educate
- Use breathing and relaxation training with hypnotic self cues.
- Invoke hypnotic images to experience the "triggers" while relaxed
- Experience the trauma through hypnotic exposure
- Integrate the entire work into a self care program that will last indefinitely
- Find new life and meaning after the healing begins

There are no guarantees for success in all cases, but many are helped by this process. Almost every person who has experienced significant trauma is capable of entering hypnotic trance and the more intense the trauma, the easier it appears to achieve trance (Spiegel, Hunt, & Dondershine, 1988). Veterans with PTSD have been found to have higher scores on measures of hypnotizability (Spiegel, Rhue, Lynn, & Kirsch, 1993; Spiegel, 1988;

Stutman & Bliss, 1985). Twenty years of research indicates that these techniques are effective and successful in helping clients overcome the lingering effects of trauma (Spiegel, et al, 1993). This is a powerful way to allow clients to face their memories in a comfortable, safe environment and learn to deal with situations in their lives now that might be associated with the traumatic memories. This assists the clients in learning that they are safe. They can undergo their distress while feeling relaxed so that it begins to decrease to a level that is tolerable or non-existent. From there, the client can reclaim their life and move on.

The cognitive approach of changing one's thinking to change one's life is important here. This is also a part of hypnotic exposure therapy. However, this is <u>not</u> directive hypnosis that is similar to cognitive-behavioral therapy, which is an umbrella term that actually includes a number of treatment approaches we will not be doing. It includes the therapies that would be called behavior therapy and cognitive therapy. They are interventions that focus on a number of main areas of human behavior. Some of those do try to reduce physiological arousal. Methods like relaxation training that attempt to induce relaxation and challenge the physiological arousal part of human behavior. Other interventions center on what people say to themselves and how they think. Behavioral approaches work on helping people change their actions, their overt behaviors, and what they say or do around other people. Finally, some of the cognitive interventions focus on helping people alter their living situations so that changes in those environments will help impact their behavior and emotions. Some of the techniques that we utilize emerge from cognitive-behavioral approaches, like anxiety management, relaxation training, and motivational enhancement methods. They are only small pieces of the whole in this method. Methods of behavioral establishment, such as getting people to go out and engage in activities in their daily life is a way of combating PTSD, goal setting, and self monitoring distress. These are all related to cognitive behavioral methods and many of these changes are instituted by directive hypnosis. But, these methods typically are treating the symptoms and not the source (the trauma).

Therefore, when we do hypnotic exposure therapy to reduce re-experiencing symptoms or reduce hyper arousal symptoms, we do not always need to focus on distress from related thinking or beliefs, as when we use a directive thought change therapy to help a veteran who is troubled by actions in the war zone. Sometimes cognitive therapists try not so much to eliminate symptoms, but to help people manage their symptoms. This might result from an improved understanding of symptoms, a better sense of what cues symptoms, and anxiety management methods. These approaches can help us deal with a lot of the other connected problems that go along with PTSD, like alcohol or substance use, social seclusion, anger management, panic management, relationship issues, and changing health behavior. So, directive hypnosis and cognitive behavioral methods can be used in many different ways as an adjunct to hypnotic exposure but are not part of hypnotic exposure. We can choose directive thought changing methods that assist the process but they are not the process itself.

The therapist-client relationship is very important. Having a good relationship is necessary for delivery of any interventions. Where there is no relationship, there is no trust, there is no safety, and there is no treatment. We must utilize a set of principles for understanding or conceptualizing the person who comes to us for assistance and a set of methods for changing emotions and behavior. But in order to deliver these particular benefits to the client, we must have a good relationship. By "good relationship", I mean an empathic therapist is going to be far more successful than a non-empathic one. We therapists need to see ourselves as educators and coaches. There must be a mutual relationship that is established to develop goals, to mutually evaluate the impact of treatment, and to collaboratively adjust where treatment is going if needed. That is the core part of any therapy.

For self care, the therapist must be strong enough to hear the story without denying the harsh reality of it or blaming the victim. The therapist must not be "freaked out" by the story that is shared. The narrative can only heal fully when heard by a trusted audience. To be trusted, the therapist must be fully prepared to experience the grief, rage, and terror that the client experienced. Listen, feel compassion, and do not judge. Remember that the client's courage needs to be mirrored by the therapist's courage. The relationship is essential to healing.

The American Psychological Association (Spiegel, et al, 1993 APA)

recommends that all hypnotic therapy follow the eight "C"s. These are:

1. <u>Confront</u> the trauma
2. <u>Condensation</u> of the experience – details unnecessary- find general aspects
3. <u>Confession</u> – guilt & shame memories

4. **Consolation** –"I am sorry this happened to you"
5. **Conscious** – bring subconscious material to surface
6. **Concentration** - mobilize and focus – ritual safety
7. **Control** – remove feelings of helplessness – self hypnosis
8. **Congruence** – acknowledge, tolerate, and work through the trauma to reintegrate self (find meaning).

I agree with all of these recommendations with the exception of condensation. The devil is in the details and often it is necessary to recall details to move beyond the experience.

Hypnotic exposure covers many areas of therapy with other names, such as prolonged exposure, flooding, or systematic desensitization (a form of exposure in which a person is exposed gradually to more and more difficult or anxiety eliciting aspects of the traumatic experience). It is important for us to remember here that the concept of hypnotic exposure and real world (in vivo) exposure are both to be used. Hypnotic exposure with trauma memories is accomplished by having clients imaginally re-experience the event. This happens as the clients tell us in emotional detail over a repeated process what occurred in their experience. The idea is that with multiple telling, the person becomes better able to tolerate the emotions which gradually decreases the stress. In vivo or real-world exposure is different. It is the process by which we encourage the person to relax themselves with auto-hypnotic techniques, then, go out and confront feared situations or triggers. They will begin to do this repeatedly until fear diminishes. This is done in a gradual way by creating a fear hierarchy, where a person takes on progressively more difficult situations or triggers in the real world. It is also recommended that a measure of distress be used to appropriately determine the effectiveness of treatment by asking clients to report their level of distress pre- and post-exposure on a scale of 1 – 100, with 100 being most distressed (Wilson, Friedman, & Lindy, 2001). Research suggests that treatment is actually more successful with the combined in office hypnotic exposure and assigned in vivo exposure to situations between sessions (Foa & Rothbaum, 2007). In summary, the treatment consists of:

- Hypnotic exposure: Confronting trauma memories repeatedly until they are no longer associated with extreme distress
- In Vivo or real-world exposure: Confronting feared situations or triggers while hypnotically relaxed, repeatedly, until fear is extinguished, often in a gradual way (i.e., anxiety/fear hierarchy)
- Combining both: Treatments are more effective if both exposures are combined

Hypnotic exposure is different than ordinary exposure therapies. The first thing that's important is the client must experience and be comfortable in the trance state. Exposure is not conducted in short increments because we need to maintain the emotional presence of the trauma memory, that is the feelings associated with the memory, long enough, for their anxiety to increase, be maintained by the experience, and then to slowly decrease. This will take some time. Typically, hypnotic exposure consists of sessions that begin with an induction of five to fifteen minutes and forty five to ninety minutes of actual exposure for a person. As therapists, we assume the role of guides. And though we can be very directive in this kind of therapy, it is not directive hypnosis. We ask open questions about sensory details of the scene, such as,"what were you seeing, smelling, hearing, and what was happening in your body?" This process assists us to increase the number of sensory cues for memory retrieval, which in turn helps clients to more successfully access their memories. We want them to seek and retrieve details of the scene. We ask them to give an account of their experiences. They should appear to be recalling the event as if it's happening now. Perhaps, they might say,"I am driving down the street. I look over and I see a pile of trash. Too late I notice the wires running from it. It is an IED." Speaking in present tense is a sign that the hypnotic exposure is working well.

This results in increased emotional access to the memory and an increase in the activation of the memory, which is important in bringing the brain into action, specifically the amygdala and hippocampus. This allows the memory to begin to be integrated into memory in a holistic way. I will talk more on this in the section concerning integration of memory. Hypnotic exposure encourages complete and focused attention to the emotional aspects of the memory. Therefore, we expose the pieces of the traumatic memory that are most associated with anxiety, psychological or physiological fear, and terror. Also, we assist the client to expose the parts of memory that are most associated with low energy or negative emotions and evaluations such as shame or guilt Therapists must be alert for emotional avoidance because we want our clients to fully experience their emotions and feelings at the time of the trauma. These are what we want the person to habituate to and reduce. One of the tools in doing that is to ask our clients to monitor their own distress and to tell us how distressed they are feeling on a rating scale.

A typical subjective distress scale (SDS) may be from 0, meaning absolutely no distress, to 10, representing extreme distress. This gives us an additional indicator with reference to whether or not we are activating the memory. Therefore, when the client rates their subjective distress as a nine or a ten out of a scale of ten, the numbers help us determine that we are getting the necessary emotional activation. Remember that our clients must remain in the exposure long enough for the anxiety to decrease. This might involve moving them into and out of the memory repeatedly while asking them to clarify the amount or rate of SDS each time. No clients should be pushed to enter the experience longer than they feel able to. We do not want them to run away from situations in vivo or from therapy. They must set the speed of the therapy. Each successful attempt should be acknowledged with empathy, care, and support. The client's courage must be noted. This is difficult work. Give the clients some well deserved appreciation for their efforts as reinforcement. If they are telling us about their trauma, we don't want them to experience extreme anxiety and flee by running out of the office. Leaving or avoiding these feelings and situations is just another symptom manifestation. We want them to remain in their memory long enough to make emotional contact with their anxiety to gradually allow it to decrease. Letting them re-experience the trauma without giving time for habituation to occur is in itself a form of abuse. They must re-experience the event long enough for the emotional distress to decrease. However, we cannot force the issue. We want them to progress through their recollections or through their visits to previously avoided situations in the real world at their own pace. We have to offer a lot of encouragement, congratulate them for the hypnotic exposures completed, and help them push themselves. Do not allow them to forget the rationale behind this treatment and help them understand how this is going to benefit them. Always acknowledge how difficult this experience is while supporting their courage and progress. Some statements that might be used are:

- "You're doing fine; stay with it."
- "You've done very well."
- "It took a lot of courage to stick it out."
- "That's right."
- "Very good."
- "I know this is difficult."
- "You're doing a good job."

Therefore, the hypnotherapist does not direct and yet has a directive role in the hypnotic exposure. We provide a powerful rationale for treatment. We assist the client to maintain focus on the "light at the end of the tunnel", that is, freedom from symptoms. The promise of feeling whole and confident again is kept in the foreground of consciousness. Never lose sight of the fact that this experience is very unpleasant for many clients. When they have decided that they are going to do this, they need to completely understand what will most likely happen. They need to understand why they are participating in the hypnotic exposure and how it's going to profit them. Frequently, the experience of many clients is a feeling that they're getting worse, not better. This appears to be a result of the treatment stopping years of emotional avoidance. We are guiding them into powerful emotional contact with their memories. These are memories that they have not been in touch with or have avoided for some time due to their emotional content. Our role is to support our clients to carry on with the process.

For that reason, we need to assist them to stay in the memory of the situation and support them to carry on in the exposure therapy. We must do all we can to prevent emotional avoidance, whether through distraction or suggested dissociation to observation of the event. We may be required to shift clients from time to time into talking about parts of the trauma experience that are not emotionally evocative or ask them to leave out certain fine points of the experience. On the other hand, we may help them to access and activate their memory by inquiring about what's happening in their body, feelings, and emotions. Sometimes, they might follow that feeling into more detailed memories of the event. At the same time, however, we also want to help them to manage their level of arousal. Under no circumstances do we want our clients to become completely overwhelmed and dissociated. We do not want them to lose their awareness of or connection to the present in such a way as it might be difficult to assist them to exit the experience if the emotional arousal becomes too intense. Some clients may require we do that by assisting them in a waking trance state where they may keep their eyes open and orient to their present surroundings if need be. In short, the benefits of client education are as follows:

- Provides a strong justification for hypnotic exposure therapy
- Aids in prevention of emotional avoidance
- Gives confidence to the client to carry on with the process

- Assists with memory access and activation
- Assists in client managing level of emotional arousal

At this point it may be helpful to outline what might happen in a typical hypnotic exposure session. In short, characteristically sessions will involve:

- 5- 15 minutes for induction
- 45-90 minutes of hypnotic exposure
- Guiding a client towards sensory details of scene to increase access to memories
  - Description of scene
  - Sensory details of scene
  - As if happening now (use first person tense to describe)
- Making sure there is focused attention to emotional aspects of memory
- Including attention to thoughts, feelings, bodily sensations
- Being alert for emotional avoidance
- Utilizing self-monitoring (SDS: "subjective distress scores")
- Ensuring clients remain in exposure long enough for anxiety to decrease
- Allowing clients to advance at their own speed
- Offering clients positive feedback and support for exposures completed and encouragement to challenge

themselves to go farther

- Acknowledging the difficulty of hypnotic exposure therapy for the client

Between sessions, in vivo exposure is very important. The therapy that combines both in vivo (real world) exposure and hypnotic exposure is likely to be more successful. Between sessions, we want our clients to make planned visits to previously avoided situations or locations while in a relaxed state. We must structure these visits to previously avoided situations very carefully. We need the clients' input to create a hierarchy of stressful situations as in systematic desensitization. Together we can create a list of distressing trigger situations from most to least distress. We need to suggest the clients approach the least distressing situations first. The hierarchy must include conditions that are really being avoided by them. Their approach must be carefully structured to make sure they are relaxed and successful. They have to be safe situations. We do not want them to enter experiences that are not objectively safe. There must be a very deliberate plan of action. The therapist and client must work together to make a systematic list of situations to be avoided. Again, we want to arrange the in vivo situations that they will approach in a hierarchy of difficulty. We give the client plain instructions to continue in the situation until their anxiety decreases. We want the clients to record their improvement on these tasks. If appropriate or possible, initially we might have the clients use a "buddy system" to help them to move toward these avoided situations and then progressively remove the social support. So, the outline of this method for real life exposure to triggering situations is:

- A detailed plan for real life exposure
  - choose locations and conditions cautiously
  - areas must be secure and harmless
- Prescribed assignments
  - Use hierarchy of distress
  - May use social support or "buddy system"
- Directions to stay in location/condition until anxiety decreases

Chapters 8- 12 Hypnotic Exposure Therapy Step by Step

"Great pain, when it is honored from the heart, opens into great understanding"

– Jack Kornfield

Chapter 8

Therapy Session 1

The initial session involves information gathering using the steps discussed in assessment. Do not begin therapy without first establishing the client's status and treatment goals as listed below:

- Determine medical status (get medical release from physician)
- Establish substance abuse status
- Screen for environmental stability
- Screen emotional stability and coping skills

  Suicide ideation

  Psychosis

- Determine the motivation level of client
- Verify social support, cooperation, and problems
- Define how he or she (the client) sees the problem.
- Find treatment goals that focus on client's needs in ways that are appropriate according to the therapist's contribution

- Establish treatment goals from the client's views, judgments, and preferences
- Discover additional problems, what led to their development, and what maintains problems
- Determine the needs of the client based on responses from client and therapist
- Build treatment goals around client needs
- Negotiate a treatment contract, along with goals and processes.

It is best to begin by providing an overview of the treatment process and the rationale behind what hypnotic exposure therapy involves. Begin with a simple introduction, such as, "Today will be our first session together and we will spend most of the session getting acquainted. I need to ask you some questions about your experiences, reactions, and emotions. However, I would like to begin by explaining the goals of hypnotic exposure therapy and describe the techniques you will be learning as we do this work together." You need to be clear about the realities of the treatment. This is going to take 8 to 15 sessions. The average is 10 sessions and most of them will last about 60 - 90 minutes. Sessions may be once or twice a week depending on the client's needs. Therapy will last about two months. We are here to focus on the fears that our clients experience. They must be informed of this approach. The fears they are experiencing are directly related to their trauma experience(s). The clients need to understand what maintains those reactions and why facing these fears is beneficial.

A central contributor to maintaining fear is avoidance. People try to avoid traumatic memories by pushing them away and by avoiding situational or environmental reminders. Because avoidance actually maintains the symptoms, the treatment is focused on helping the client to stop avoidance by confronting the trauma-related thoughts and situations. All of this should be addressed directly to the client as described here. This treatment involves using hypnosis to allow the client to imagine the traumatic experience while in a deeply relaxed state. We might say to our clients, "Therefore, you will be asked to recall the trauma situation while in this state. This is found to be very effective in reducing PTSD symptoms". Then, explain how they will be asked to work on their own at home with "in vivo exposure" assignments. This just means they will be taught to self relax and gradually confront situations that have created fear in the past. As they gradually enter into these "triggers" while very relaxed, they can begin to understand that they are not truly dangerous and can be effectively "handled". Then, ask the client if he or she understands the rationale and if this makes sense to them. You may even wish to create a "rationale" handout for clients to take home and read.

The next part of the session requires information gathering. We need to identify the presenting problems, the client's functioning, the trauma itself, physical/mental health, social support, and alcohol/drug use. Also, there must be a "target" trauma if the client has suffered multiple traumas. After completing the trauma interview, the session should be concluded by an initial hypnotic induction and relaxation breathing exercise. The goal is to have our client experience this relaxed state and have a post-hypnotic cue with which to enter this state on his or her own (See initial relaxation script in Appendix 1). I strongly suggest that the initial relaxation be recorded and given to the client for home use. There are very effective digital recording devices available for purchase that one may use to record a relaxation session. These can simply be connected to a computer by jump drive and the recording downloaded for future use as a CD or MP3 file. It is also recommended that the client be instructed to complete the relaxation two to three times daily until the next session. A typical relaxation session should only be 15 – 20 minutes and this should be easy to use at home.

My initial therapeutic specialty was a motivational interviewing approach. This technique, as specific to substance abuse, is described in detail by Miller and Rollnik (2002). I strongly suggest that any professional who is interested in motivating others read this book. In my opinion, combining motivational interviewing and hypnosis, two of the most powerful techniques for change that have ever been utilized, is a guarantee for therapeutic success. When we initially interview our clients, they may be somewhat reluctant to initiate the processes of hypnotic exposure therapy. Fear of reliving the trauma is a natural reaction. It is also strongly indicated in maintaining symptoms. Our clients may feel that they are "damned if they do and damned if they don't". We need to increase their motivation to begin the therapy process to ensure success.

In the first session, we need to identify as many disruptions and dissatisfactions they have in life right now. Then, we must make the client aware of the potential for positive results as a direct result of the hypnotic therapy, not the least of which is symptom removal and reduction. We need to identify all potential obstacles to success. Clients that do not participate by regular attendance, completing homework, using their home relaxation recordings/cues, or actively engaging in the "in vivo" exercises, will fail.

In the appendix section, I have included some motivational assignments that may be useful in increasing client compliance to treatment protocols or simply finding information to use in more directive hypnotic sessions. The focus is on reporting what is wrong or what needs to change to improve their lives. At the same time, we want to know what they need to do more of to feel more joy and meaning in life. Those would be the goals for treatment completion (See Appendix 2). This is often very important as Watkins (1949) explained that with good knowledge of the client's motivational structure, skillfully presented suggestion and persuasion are more successful in working with PTSD.

We might simply ask what activities or situations they are presently not participating in with family and friends because of their symptoms. What are things that they no longer have interest in that gave them pleasure before? What new things would they like to accomplish? How do they want their lives to be different or better? How will their lives be changed when therapy is finished?

We need to know of previous attempts to get better. What have they tried before? What worked? How did it help? What happened then? What was not so good? What may get in the way of their completing work on their own? What is better in their life since the trauma that they want to remain? And, one of my favorite motivating questions, "What will change if you don't do therapy?" The clients know that if they do nothing, then nothing will change. Sometimes, a person just needs someone to bring

this to conscious awareness.

"To confront a person with their own shadow is to show them their own light"

- Carl Jung

Chapter 9
Therapy Session 2

Always begin by checking in with the client for a personal update. Then, ask about the success of relaxation. Always frame this as "Tell me about your success with relaxing." Process this information and negotiate any technique changes that might improve relaxation. It is very important at this time to develop of hierarchy of distressing situations from least upsetting to most upsetting. This requires clear communication and negotiation. The focus is on activities, environments, or situations of avoidance. Suppose the client becomes very symptomatic at the sight of sand. We may need to start with a picture of sand for in vivo exposure homework and work up to a trip to the beach or desert later on. These are to be approached following self relaxation. The goal is to enter or face the fear while relaxed in order to find that safety is possible. These small successes will promote client confidence. This will be the homework between sessions or the in vivo experiences. In these assignments the places of avoidance are rated and approached systematically to reduce symptoms.

It will be good to explain to the client a list of common reactions to trauma. Many of the common changes are "normal" and many fade in one to three months or so. However, those that remain after that time are most likely symptomatic of PTSD. These common reactions will be:

- Fear – Certain cues will trigger anxiety. These may be certain places, smells, time of day, or noises, etc. The clients must note the times of day, certain places, people, activities, smells, noises when they are feeling afraid and list possible triggers.
- Re-experiencing – The client's mind may be attempting to get rid of the traumatic memories by forcing the process into consciousness. These become unwanted or intruding thoughts. They may have flashbacks, that is, the experience of visual pictures of some aspect of the trauma suddenly entering into their mind or through nightmares of the event.
- Increased arousal – Clients may be experiencing shakiness or jitters. Certain stimuli or situations may create an exaggerated startle response. Often, some persons will have a difficult time focusing or concentrating. There may be a sense of irritability, possibly due to lack of sleep or hyper-vigilance. Finally, the client may suffer from continued flight or fight response. The sense of being constantly "on alert" can have the effect of constant stress response leading to increases in adrenal activity and cortisol production. This in turn may result in decreased immune functioning and frequent physical illness.
- Avoidance or Numbness – As we discussed at length in the chapter concerning cognitions and treatment. The client may avoid environmental stimuli and "triggers" that cue emotional responses. This may actually reinforce the PTSD symptoms. Also, if clients believe they cannot be safe at all and cannot relax, the ultimate avoidance might

be complete emotional shutdown. They may prefer to feel nothing rather than constant threat. Also, clients may find that they have no interest in activities that they used to enjoy. This is another example of shutting down.

- Anger or Irritability – Anger often results from a sense of betrayal but not always. The idea that the world or God is not fair or just can result in feelings of chronic anger. Clients' behaviors may indicate a general statement to others that they should fear the client. This could be used as a "wall of protection". The clients may dislike feeling fear so much that they want to ensure that others fear them.
- Guilt and Shame – This is pure and simple self blame. Our clients might feel that what they did at the time of trauma was not enough. Clients may wonder and ruminate as to what they could have done differently or done more of to prevent the trauma. Often, this is greatest among those in authority or victims who feel responsible for what happened.
- Grief and Depression – Many clients will feel down and depressed. This sense of intense sadness or hopelessness indicates depression. They may despair to the point of self harm or suicide. Trauma survivors may experience a profound sense of loss. They may feel the loss of who they once were, of friends/comrades, safety, life/time, or loss of innocence. Grief is a natural reaction to loss of any kind.
- Negative Self Image or World View – The internal view of self or the world in general may become skewed towards a focus on the negative. The clients may see themselves as weak or stupid. The might believe that they deserve to

suffer. They may believe that both they and the world are not to be trusted. They are "bad" and so are others. No one or no thing is safe. As a result, interpersonal relationships will also suffer.

- Substance Abuse – A client may have turned to alcohol or drug use to aid in the coping. This may be a technique to avoid or numb feelings. It may also be a way to avoid memories that result in an increase of trauma symptoms.
- Connection of Reactions – As you may have already noted, a lot of these reactions are interrelated. Many of these trauma reactions will occur together, and "feed" off of one another to increase symptoms. They may combine to make the overall reactions more intense or more frightening. However, our clients must understand that as they progress through treatment it is precisely because of the interrelated reactions that all symptoms should become less and less distressing.

Next it will be wise to explain to the client in detail the theory behind in vivo exposure. As mentioned previously, this involves the client making planned visits to previously avoided situations or locations while in a relaxed state. This requires careful planning. We must work together to create a hierarchy of stressful situations. We create an ordered list of upsetting trigger situations from most to least distressing. First, the clients must approach the least distressing situations. We need to structure the process in order to make sure they are relaxed and successful. We want them to enter safe situations with a deliberate plan of action.

Begin by simply asking the client to remember that it is common for persons with PTSD to avoid memories, thoughts, and emotions. This provides temporary relief but in the long run makes symptoms worse. If the clients can express understanding of this principle, namely that avoidance increases PTSD suffering, then ask them to give you examples of how they personally use these avoidance tactics. Maybe, they used to enjoy vacationing at the beach. Now, they plan to vacation in the mountains to avoid sand. The sand triggers memories of a trauma that occurred in the desert and so it is to be avoided. By using in vivo exposure between sessions, the client may learn to gradually approach sand while relaxed and eventually return to the beach feeling secure again.

For example, the clients first relax and approach a place with sand. Next, nothing harmful happens. The clients have then confronted a situation that was previously avoided because they thought it was dangerous or evoked distressing feelings. The clients learn this is safe and they no longer have to avoid it. After all, if you never approach the sand, you never find that it is safe. Third, many clients believe that if they stay in the feared situation, their distress will escalate out of control. By staying with the experience long enough, they can find their fear begins to diminish. As a result of this success, the clients' self esteem increases. They begin to feel competent again. They can return to more normal functioning. The end result is a decline in symptoms and a feeling of confidence in their own ability to cope. This is empowering for our clients and helps to reduce the erroneous thoughts that may lead to dependence on the therapist to solve the problem.

From a cognitive view, the ability to move into these situations allows the client to relive memories fully, changing the memory from sensory to verbal processing. This helps to create the full narrative within their mind. Then, the client can address more personal and transpersonal issues concerning giving the experience meaning. Reliving in thought is not dangerous. He or she can approach these situations without fear. They can handle it, just like the example of being thrown from a horse. They can now get up in the saddle again. Their fear is now greatly diminished. Remember, the client must be clear on the difference between these small excursions on their own and the extended exposure to the trauma they will experience in hypnosis. The two experiences will work together in removing symptoms but they are approached from two different directions.

Let's take a moment to discuss the subjective distress scores. The subjective distress score is a method for clients to express in measurable terms how upset they are in any given situation. This will give the therapist a quantitative measure of upset and success. Most of these scales are on a rating of 100 to 0. It is a fairly simple method; the higher the number the larger the distress. It is best to explain this to clients immediately following your talk on in vivo exposure so they can begin to rate possible situations on the scale. Then, we can work together on the hierarchy we need for success.

You may tell the client, "In order to discover exactly how much distress or discomfort you experience in certain situations, we will use a scale that we call the Subjective Distress Scale (SDS). For our purposes, I like to use a simpler scale from 10 to 0. If you were to rate your distress at 10, that would communicate to me that you were extremely distressed. This would be on par with the most upset you have ever been in your life. Zero indicates no distress at all or possibly a completely relaxed feeling. Most people who express distress of 10 will be experiencing physical reactions indicating extreme anxiety, such as increased heart rate, shallow breath, or sweating palms. For each person this may be different but a score of 10 would indicate powerful distress. For example, if we were standing on a cliff and I was afraid of heights but you were not, I might go to 10 while you may be relaxed. That is why it is a subjective, individual measure."

In order to be sure that we have a personalized SDS, it should be covered in this session. Ask clients directly about what types of situations they avoid and what situations are relaxing. For a veteran who experienced an IED destroying a vehicle they were traveling in, you may come up with something like: laying in bed = 0; talking with spouse = 2; going to the beach = 5; trash = 7; talking with other vets = 7; driving = 10. Then, situations can be investigated further. Which beach is most stressful? Where do you have the greatest distress when driving? What specifically about trash makes the distress more powerful? At that point we are ready to begin making a detailed hierarchy. As treatment continues, both of you may discover items to add to the list. In the beginning, try to keep the list to no more than five due to time constraints and ask the client to identify more on the handout you will provide for homework (See Appendix 3).

There are three main types of situations that are avoided by clients with PTSD. First, there are the situations that in the client's mind are very dangerous. Keep in mind, these are situations that they perceive as dangerous and may not be so. The ones that we can identify as relatively safe are the only ones we can recommend for real life exposure because we want to have a zero risk for anything harmful to happen. The clients believe that they will be harmed but the risk is merely in their subjective experience. Second, there are the situations that are reminders of the trauma. These are much like classical conditioned responses. The clients are exposed to similar colors, odors, or sounds that may have been present during the trauma so that the distress response is cued. It may be something as simple as watching the news. These triggers are perceived as inherently dangerous. It is the memory and emotions they cue that are avoided. Finally, there may be activities that the clients used to enjoy and they have no longer shown any interest in them. They have effectively withdrawn from the world. We must use this work to get them involved in enjoyable activities again.

The distressing situations that are avoided may come in a variety of types. Below is a short list of typically avoided situations or triggers for veterans:

1. Driving a vehicle or being stopped at a light
2. Reading war news or watching the news on TV
3. Talking with someone about the trauma
4. Experiencing unexpected loud noises
5. Seeing other veterans
6. Acknowledging military holidays such as Memorial Day or Veteran's Day
7. Remembering anniversary dates
8. Watching war or action movies
9. Going to places with similar environments (sand, etc.)
10. Visiting the VA hospital

Remember that in vivo exposure starts with situations that

produce moderate stress. After success at that level, there is a gradual progression to more severely distressing situations. Each situation may have an adjustment factor that allows one to lower the amount of stress. For instance, the location or time of day may be changed to reduce SDS. The clients need to plan on being in the situation for about 30 minutes and they should still be experiencing some stress. There should not be complete relief. A reduction of 50% in SDS is about right. Careful attention should be placed on the decision of where to go first so that chances for success are maximized. Discussion with the client about experiences of previous success can assist in motivation to begin and continue with the process. Finally, always work with the clients to agree on two or more possible real life exposure situations so there are options for beginning the work. Reinforce the idea that they must not leave the situation until they feel a decrease in distress in order for the assignments to work effectively.

"Where to begin? Let's start with the end. This black and white photo don't capture the skin. From the shock of a shell or the memory of smell, If red is for Hell; the war was in color"

– Carbon Leaf from "War Was In Color" on Love, Loss, Hope, Repeat CD

Chapter 10

Therapy Session 3

The real work has begun. The clients have been practicing self hypnosis relaxation at home and have been involved in their own recovery by completing their in vivo exposure assignments. Begin by checking in and seeing how things have been since the last visit. There should be quite a bit of time reserved at the beginning of the session for processing the real life exposure assignments. Focus on successes or any positive change in patterns of distress. Praise, praise, praise! Remind the client of the rationale behind the approach. Discuss with the client again how these confronting exercises will help to overcome PTSD symptoms. Talk again about the benefits of getting in touch with what actually happened, how it is important for the client to recall the thoughts and feelings that actually occurred. Remind the client of the benefits of habituation and the resulting decrease in distress. Then, explain that the client will be revisiting the trauma through hypnosis during this session. The clients need to know that they will be doing this memory work for about 45 – 60 minutes so they can properly prepare.

Remind clients that they may approach the memory gradually, at their own pace. The therapist is not going to be directive for the first session. Instead, we will focus on being calm and supportive throughout the initial experience. The client should be allowed to determine the amount of detail with which to recall the event for this session. If the client has experienced more than one trauma, it might be most helpful to focus on the most distressing first. Then, the less distressing memories are more easily dealt with in the future. However, if clients are very resistant to the idea of approaching the most distressing memory, allow them to decide on what they feel they can mange. Initially, it may be most important to get over the less upsetting aspects of the trauma. We want success in the earlier stages to create the expectation of continued success and confidence for the work to come. Warn the client that sometimes things may get worse before getting better. That is, the first exposures to the memory may bring about a lot of distress but through habituation and relaxation, things will improve. Also, the clients may need to be reminded that no matter how hard they have tried to not think of the memory, it has returned in some form to haunt them and cause distress. Therefore, the process of entering the memory is critical in the relief of symptoms. It may be like eating some spoiled food. It will upset your stomach. You must digest it and get it out of you to find relief. Reliving the memory is like digesting it and being free of its negative effects.

The entering and processing of traumatic memory is a potent opportunity for learning. The crisis invites us to emerge from the habitual patterns of thinking and doing in order to create a new sense of wholeness. The client may often emerge with new insights useful for integration and healing. Processing after the hypnosis session allows any new awareness to become more explicit. The client can begin to modify his or her cognitions while creating more positive expectations. It is important that they do not leave the session stressed or anxious. Reiterate the idea that this emotional processing of distressing memories is the beginning of healing. If clients become very anxious, they may wish to bring someone along for emotional support, especially on the way home.

After all of these possible concerns are addressed, it is time to begin the hypnotic exposure. It is best to use the standard induction for this session that has been used for hypnotic relaxation. Once trance has been acquired, there are a few methods for entering the trauma memory. One, the client is invited to experience the negative emotional sensation and follow it back through time to the source. This is a sort of coached abreaction. Second, the client may be asked directly to imagine the event as it occurred. Three, the therapist may suggest a time line that the client may follow back to the source of their difficulties. Finally, there is an approach where it is suggested that the client imagine themselves in a theater of sorts where the trauma may be observed safely in detail as if on a movie screen. Each of these methods will be described here in detail. It is the choice of the client and therapist as to which will be appropriate in each individual's case.

Remember, all hypnosis is self hypnosis. The clients will be taking themselves back to the traumatic memory. The therapist is their guide and assistant. It is happening with the client's psyche. All sessions should be audio taped or digitally recorded for the client and therapist to review later. If appropriate, based on the therapist's evaluation of the client's current ability, the client may take the recording home and review it as part of an ongoing relaxed exposure.

Before beginning, it may be useful to set a relaxation anchor with the client. This can aid in confidence during the session because it provides an "escape hatch". The relaxation anchor is an image, cue, or hypnotic suggestion that may be used to pull the client out of the memory rapidly into a comfortable, relaxed, and safe place. I must add a warning here. The client needs to stay in the distress long enough to lessen the distress. By using an escape anchor, you may be promoting the avoidance we are trying to eliminate. I do not use this method but some may be more comfortable with it. I am confident that I can bring the client out of distress with a few simple relaxation suggestions. The hypnotic exposure begins with the induction. Then, we will use one of the regression models to return to the trauma event. Keep in mind that counting is not necessary. Any of the approaches will work without the use of counting numbers.

Let us begin with the abreaction approach. First described by Freud and Jung in a simple form, this method is very effective for returning the client to the trauma memory while in hypnosis. This is an associated form of hypnosis. The client is returned to the trauma by following the emotional affect to the source. The client will be "in" the memory. If the client would prefer to begin as an observer, this is not the approach to use. While in trance, the client is asked to feel the negative emotions described during the initial interviews. Once he or she has connected to the feeling, the client is simply asked to subjectively return to the source of that emotional response. "You are in a comfortable, safe, and relaxed place now. Imagine vividly the feelings you have described that are distressing for you. Locate the feeling and allow yourself to return to the first time you felt it." Often, this suggestion is all that is needed. However, it may be helpful to assist with some simple instructions such as, "I am going to count from one to three. Simply allow your mind to wander and drift back through time. When I reach the number three, you will find yourself at the time and place where these feelings began. One, ... following the feeling, drifting gently back to its source. Two, ...leaving now behind, floating back over time. And three, ...You have returned to the source of these feelings." Then, the therapist will begin with standard questioning techniques.

- "What are you aware of?"
- "What happens next?"
- "What are you experiencing?"
- "What might be important for you to remember now?"

Always use open ended questions. Never use leading or guiding questions that might interfere with the details of the actual memory. Allow clients to remain in the memory long enough to demonstrate a noticeable reduction in discomfort as revealed by their physical appearance or change in the emotional content of verbal responses.

Remember to utilize ego strengthening techniques for praising the client's courage and determination for success, such as:

- "That's right (or very good), stay with the image."
- "You've done very well."
- "You are very courageous to stick it out."
- "Stay with your feelings; you are doing very well."
- "I know this is difficult but you are succeeding."
- "You're doing a good job."

- "Stay with the image; you are safe here."
- "You're doing fine"

These questions and ego strengthening techniques may be used in any of the hypnotic exposure techniques mentioned hereafter. Following an acceptable period of time, the client should be returned to the present and the session processed. You may care to end the session with some healing suggestions, such as, "In the future, you'll notice that you find yourself feeling safer, worrying less, and focusing more on the enjoyable parts of life." This is not necessary but may be helpful for some clients. Then, you may use the "reorienting to present process" outline at the end of the induction found in the appendix.

It would be good at this time to begin to process the first hypnotic exposure experience. The art of "digesting" the trauma is facilitated by the therapist. The client may now begin to organize the memory, separate the past from the present, reduce anxiety, and separate the event from the "triggers". We are seeking forgotten details, future solutions, safety, strengths, meaning, or anything that might be used to integrate the memories. The client may be asked questions to facilitate this, such as:

- "Are there forgotten details that have returned to you, such as, remembering who was saved or who was lost?"
- "Are there ideas for a better future? What does the solution look like, sound like, feel like?"
- "How can you describe or imagine the future would be with this no longer holding you back?"
- "Was there a time when you felt safe?"

- "What strengths do you have that have helped you survive?"
- "What do you believe are the lessons that can be taken from your experience?"
- "What part of you was lost or left behind? What would it say to you or you to it? What could help to be whole again?"

Now, we also want to measure the subjective distress of the client. Self-monitoring forms (SDS: "subjective distress scores") for measuring anxiety or fear on scale of 0 – 10 from least to worst are useful both before and after sessions. They may be used as a measure of treatment success. This may also increase clients' self confidence as they acknowledge that there is an improvement in their thoughts or feelings of distress. So, at the very least, we need to obtain this number from our clients after the initial exposure session. This will be our baseline for improvement measures. In following sessions, the client will be returned to the memory more than once and we will measure the SDS each time to monitor for habituation responses.

We need to begin to focus the client on solutions following the first exposure. Some other questions we may need to ask can be scripted into our session exit interview:

1. "How do you view the trauma now?"
2. "How does this view make you feel?"
3. "What other views might be possible?"
4. "What would you say to a loved one or friend who viewed it this way?"

5. "What would you say to someone who had a similar experience?"
6. "What does this mean to you that you had to experience this?"
7. "What does this whole experience mean to you now after the hypnotic session?"
8. "What does all of this say about you as a person?"
9. "What is the meaning of you having PTSD; why you?"

Ask the client for any questions or concerns. Discuss any changes in the homework. Set the next appointment and process the session in your own experience.

Now, let's return to other methods. If the client has demonstrated low distress during the session, it may have been that he or she was "not in the memory" and became an observer of the event. An objectively low distressed client may find more rapid benefit from one of the associated "in the memory" approaches. If the client's eyes remain open, he or she may be in extreme distress. In that case, we might rather use an observer or dissociated approach.

The second method of entering hypnotic exposure is suggesting to the client to return directly to the past traumatic event. In this situation, it is best if clients declare that they do have memory of the event, however vague it may be. Instead of mentioning the feeling involved, the client is directed to the event. "I am going to count from one to three and when I reach the number three you will find that you have returned to (whatever the event). One ..... your mind is drifting into the past (pause). Two, moving further back and more relaxed. And, three, you are now there and can recall the entire experience." Then, you would simply continue as above to complete the session.

Third, if the client is truly unsure of where to go or what to do with the process, then the appropriate method is totally non-directive in the sense that we do not know what memory we are attempting to recall. This may be associated or dissociated in the psyche when recalled, but will be firmly in the implicit or unconscious realm of memories. This method is a simple regression hypnosis approach where the client is merely directed to go to the source of the difficulty, wherever that may be in the past. "Imagine a direction that your mind may travel to retrieve memories. Possibly, there is a line that extends from the present into the past or forward to the future. This would be your timeline. Allow yourself to drift free now. Drifting free of here and now. Allow your mind to drift towards the past. We are going to return to the event that has been causing your distress. I will count from one to three and when I reach the number three you will return to the memory you need to understand your current situation. One, floating back in time (pause). Two, drifting to the exact place and time you need to be aware of for your recovery. Three, drifting to the source of your distress, NOW." Then, you may continue with the questions listed previously.

The final approach is a dissociative method. This method should be used as a beginning approach for clients who are in extreme distress. It is also considered by some to be a rapid approach to healing trauma. I do not recommend any rapid use of any treatment with this population. True healing takes time and effort. To use a one-session approach is to make the same mistake that was made in Freud and Jung's time. Simply reviewing the trauma is not enough for complete healing.

This method is presented in detail by Bandler (1985) as the "Fast Phobia Cure". Using dissociation, we may be able to rapidly remove the negative emotional impact of trauma while conserving the memory. This method has a strong visual component, and though many persons are primarily visual encoders of memory, it will not work effectively for those who primarily use auditory or kinesthetic memory.

Due to the possibility of extreme distress, it may be useful to set a relaxation anchor before beginning the session using this method. Have the clients associate with the peaceful, safe, and relaxation place. Then, set up the cue that will be used to bring them there if needed. Again, I do not use the anchoring method but some are more comfortable with it. If clients appear to be extremely distressed, I have found that a simple command to stand up will often disengage them from the trauma memory.

Begin by helping the client to understand that a one time experience can result in immediate learning. Ask the client to recall any example of one time learning in memory. Often, a client may be able to recall a time when one taste of food or drink led to a powerful learning experience. The trauma is often an example. One exposure resulted in learning of the symptomatic responses. This creates a mindset of one session learning for success which can be very useful in rapid healing. After the induction, have the client imagine a blank movie screen. Have them place an image of themselves on the screen, preferably in black and white. Make this an image of them just before the trauma occurred when they felt safe, normal, and secure. Then, dissociate the client again so that they find themselves in the movie projection booth. Have them see themselves both seated in the theater and on the screen. Pause here and allow the double dissociation to become clear and accurate for them. Now, have the client run a black and white movie of the trauma all the way through to the end of the event. Clients are then watching themselves watching a movie and removing the emotional content from the memory. They must run the movie all the way to a point where they feel safe and secure again. If they are still distressed while watching the movie, have them move the screen further away by increasing the size of the theater. Once the client has completed the movie to a safe place, have them freeze the image and erase it. Then, allow them to leave the projection booth and return to their body seated in the theater. Check with them to be sure they are doing exactly what you are suggesting. Then, ask them to run the movie backwards and in color. Watch for rapid eye movement to confirm. Repeat the process of entering the body, blanking out the picture and running the movie backwards until the client reports less than three on their SDS. Then, through hypnotic suggestion have the client move forward in time to a situation that has triggered a distress reaction, such as the beach. Ask them to imagine being there and report their feelings. There should be little or no distress. This method is best used with extremely distressed individuals. Their in vivo assignments should become rapidly successful if the method works correctly.

Any of the methods described can be very effective. If the client is doing their relaxation exercises, in vivo work, and attending their appointments, there should be noticeable changes beginning after the third session. This first hypnotic exposure session is very important. Afterwards, the client must not be distressed. Remind them that the memory is over and the office is a safe place. Provide support and calming. Normalize the reactions they might be having. Praise the client for their effort and courage. Bring any habituation responses to the client's attention. Pay attention to any symptoms that are reduced (note SDS decline). Discuss the homework between sessions and end the session.

"Something we were withholding made us weak until we found it was ourselves"

– Robert Frost

Chapter 11

Therapy Sessions 4 – 9 or "Hot Spots" Sessions

This session might be the last or there may be more work required. The client's report of successes is the key. The mind is a garden. It is fertile ground for healthy or unhealthy thoughts and emotions. We have been working to remove deep rooted weeds of distress. The time is now to determine if the healthy seeds are taking root. We begin with the SDS scales that the client takes home. If the recordings are below three on all measures we may need to move directly to discussion of meaning and termination. If the scores are still high, then we must note those that are lower and ask the client to speculate on what is working and what is not. It is again important to note any areas where habituation is occurring. Successes are noted and failures dismissed as merely needing a bit more time. We need to keep the client focused on what is better. We are changing the mind from a garden of distress to a garden of hope and joy. It requires tending.

These sessions are needed if our clients have been reluctant to remember details or shown little reduction in their subjective distress. We will direct them to remember more details of what they are seeing, hearing, smelling, and feeling. We want a detailed recollection. We are searching for what is missing that will complete the memory so that it can be fully integrated into the psyche. No more avoidance. You may want begin here to ask for SDS scores every ten minutes and record them. Ask them to acknowledge your questions as quickly as possible without leaving the memory. If it is in their memory, ask them to just say it without taking time to think or analyze their response. Continue with recall until SDS numbers decrease.

We are now concerned with identifying and removing "Hot Spots". These are the most distressing current memories. By now, the client will have most likely covered all of the least distressing parts of the trauma memory. It is time to work on those that are most avoided. These are the "Hot Spots". Ask the client to remember that they are having success in lowered distress. Because of this, we no longer need to completely recall all of the memory. Those parts that are no longer very distressing can be ignored. We want detailed exposure to the more distressing memories now. The client can advise us on what memories we need to be the focus of treatment. We are ready to reduce the memory's effects. Center on each "Hot Spot" until their distress is lessened. Then, we can return to recalling the entire event. Once this is accomplished, we may end the session and process the information as before. We continue with this approach until we are sure there are no more "Hot Spots" and the trauma is recalled completely with little or no distress (SDS 3 or less).

One method that may be used to increase the success of this phase of treatment is what I like to call "Clearing Rooms". If we compare memories to rooms in a house, we can direct the client through each room. In the room, the client can perform whatever task they feel is needed to clear or integrate the memory. This follows the psychoanalytic approach of a house being symbolic of the person. Each "Hot Spot" can be assigned its own room. For instance, a room may be in flames and the client can use any method to put out the fire. The room can be hot or cold and a thermostat can be used to adjust the temperature. Or, the client may be asked to return to a time when the house was whole or normal. Then, the client can bring that memory of wholeness to the present. There are many ways to accomplish this method. I recommend a non-directive approach that allows the client to create his or her own home/rooms and clear them as the client sees fit.

Another method is the use of lights or candles imagery. The clients may be directed to imagine the "hot" memories as lights or candles. When ready, they may approach the lights and disconnect them. Or, they might simply extinguish the candles as needed. These methods are useful only if the clients feel them to be appropriate. It is often just as effective to continue to remember the "Hot Spots" while relaxed until they do not illicit a SDS response greater than three.

We are now ready to move to terminating sessions and a processing of meaning that leads to true healing. This results in the ability to turn post traumatic stress into post traumatic strength. The warrior/hero is now ready to return to life with the knowledge acquired during therapy. Often, they can use their abilities and strengths to be of service to others. Whatever the case, they will be more whole and healthy, their memories no longer feared or avoided.

"The word hero needs to be reserved for the man or woman who is willing to take the solitary journey to the depths of the self, to re-own the shadow, to exorcise the ancient warrior psyche, to discover the power and authority of wholeness"

– Sam Keen

Chapter 12

Final Sessions: The Transpersonal - Integration & Meaning

The transpersonal approach to trauma involves the integration of myth and meaning beyond the boundaries of the personal ego. This involves a return to wholeness within oneself while remaining in touch with the archetypal realm of psyche. Trauma may result in the feeling that the self is falling to pieces as one dissociates. However, the dissociated parts of self may circle us just as the planets circle the sun. So, we may have descended into the "dark night of the soul" or become lost in that "dark wood" as we have separated parts of self. But, the very act of falling apart has assisted us to remember to transcend the self. Emerging from the ashes of our former lives, we might actually become more whole. Trauma took us to the transpersonal and we return as renewed and integrated humans.

Therefore, in the final transpersonal session(s), we may assist the return to wholeness from a meaningful, mythological experience. There are some issues we need to be aware of here. First, not all clients are ready to benefit from this final step and it must be their choice to explore this path. Having completed the standard hypnotic exposure therapy, many clients might prefer to find their own way back to wholeness. A final session simply discussing what clients take from their experience or what the entire experience has meant to them might be all that is required

They answer the questions: "How do you view the trauma now? What other views might be possible? What does this experience mean to you? What have you learned from having PTSD?" Then, they are ready to move on. Maybe, all they needed was to move beyond their PTSD symptoms. However, some clients will benefit greatly with continued assistance in exploring experiential meaning. Some may refer to this as traumatic growth.

We might begin ourselves by regarding the numerous archetypes surrounding war. In the history of Post Traumatic Stress we briefly discussed these archetypes as we referred to the Gods/Goddesses of War and the tales of Homer. Our "civilized" history is filled with tales of war. Around the world, warfare has reached monstrous and omnipresent magnitude. Aggressive energies create deep suspicion and fear. The hero/warrior archetype lives on. We must accept and integrate the warrior or like any repressed or denied energy, it will rise from the unconscious to make our lives more difficult. If we raise loud and hostile voices against it, we simply invoke its presence.

In many ways, American society seems to worship the war/warrior archetype. How else could movies like *Rambo, Full Metal Jacket, Apocalypse Now, Terminator,* or *Die Hard* (to name a very few) become so popular? As mentioned earlier, the history of civilization is defined in large part by our wars. In the past century, our whole planet was threatened by two world-wide conflicts. The end result brought us "The Cold War" and the ominous threat of a third world conflict using weapons that might destroy the entire planet. It seems that the archetype of war is a basic building block in our collective psyche.

Traditions of war and warriors appear world wide. There

have been warrior traditions through the entire human history. In India, the Kshatriya conquered and stabilized their area of the Asian continent so that it eventually became a world spiritual center. The warlike Hebrew tribes followed Yahweh, a warrior God, in their quest to conquer much of their known world. Under the stewardship of King David, these warrior virtues became the ethical code and religion for their entire civilization. There were the Roman Emperor-Warrior-Philosophers, such as Marcus Aurelius, who prior to his murder set a precedent for ethical, stoic behaviors and the expansion of civilized ideals, thus beginning a Western story of change that became the Western History of the World. Or, the story of a tiny band of Spartans who turned back the Persian Empire and most likely preserved Democracy for future generations. In America, the Native Americans have proud, honorable warrior beliefs. Also, the Samurai of Japan have honorable, disciplined, and loyal warrior traditions encompassing their culture and way of life. Muhammad was a warrior/prophet. Islam is built from war to wage jihad against evil as their religion defines it.

The warrior energy has appeared universal, especially among men and the civilizations they form. But, as easily as it can be a defense for values, it can go horribly astray. PTSD is merely one of numerous negative results. In finding meaning, we must find a way to balance the energy of the God of War so that the warrior might find stability and peace.

As mentioned before, the warrior embodies the most powerful transpersonal commitment. His loyalty is to something even more important than his life. His commitment to "might for right" goes beyond personal benefit. All personal relationships are relative and less central in the face of this transpersonal commitment. Lofty ideals of service to God, Country, King/ Queen, Democracy, Communism, Islam, or Freedom can alter the focus of life so that personal concerns no longer matter much. Thus, when feeling lost or betrayed by those ideals, trauma is much harder to bear.

Not all who fight in wars are true warriors. If being a warrior is no more than a job, then the person is just a mercenary. The warrior becomes one of those who are defined as a killer for hire. A true warrior kills in service of the greater transpersonal order. Those who thought the military life was just a job are more vulnerable to PTSD symptoms.

So, our veteran has returned from the abyss. The hypnotic exposure has worked to remove symptoms. Now, what does the warrior live for? The mission may be over. The warrior needs to move forward. New purpose and meaning are essential to constellate the archetypal self back into wholeness. The veteran needs a new personal myth to live by.

The military is constructed in an effort to maintain order in the face of the chaos of war. The Army, Navy, Air Force, or Marine Corps are archetypal entities in and of themselves. They are the embodiment of death in a cloak of morality, rule, and order. Veterans have been warriors for what is right and good. Their moral strength is so powerful that the warriors can be motivated to march into certain death. What effects occurred if the trauma makes it seem as if the moral order has been betrayed? How do we heal?

In the myth of the *Iliad,* Achilles represents the betrayed hero. He saw clearly the right of things and how his commander Agamemnon betrayed him by taking his prize of war. In Vietnam, we left defeated after winning every major battle. The feelings of dishonor and betrayal were incredibly powerful among those veterans. We have yet to see the end of our current conflicts. But as they have not yet truly ended in victory, those who are suffering and have suffered from PTSD await to see how final honors are bestowed. Coming home with honor is essential to mental health. The feeling of being appreciated without betrayal makes the transition easier and PTSD less likely to occur.

Bereavement and its proper expression are also essential to the transpersonal feeling of honor. Our government's current hiding of the dead from public view might increase the feelings of disrespect or dishonor for the valiant dead. This strikes at the core of the warrior archetype and his healthy re-integration. What happens when the warriors are struck by the destruction of their ambitions, ideals, and social world? An attitude of emotional distance or not caring for self and others results in moving further from the safety of the archetype. This in turn makes our warrior more vulnerable to the inner demons of PTSD. If one is taught that the emotions of love and grief no longer amount to anything, how can we expect our warriors to return to us in anything but an "inhuman" condition? The "enemy" too must be dehumanized, monstrous, treacherous, and evil. They must not be seen as the children of women. What happens when our warriors find themselves mirrored by the behavior of the enemy? The self loathing can be immense. Honor must be restored to the enemy in order to honor oneself. This is a part of our transpersonal integration, the restoration of honor to all concerned.

There are no enemies within or without when the process

is complete. None of our soldiers have ever thrown themselves on a grenade for self. The question for us transpersonally is how to restore the hero or the warrior with honor or fullness in the returning veteran. They need to return to the feeling of "fight for right". The war may have consumed the persons they were once. But, as the archetypal image of The Tower in the tarot deck portrays the power of destruction such as war, the security of the past has crumbled. Nothing is spared in the powerful fire. Yet, we may emerge more whole and restored. Times of pain and desperation can initiate far reaching inner transformation for the better. We may emerge from this fruitful darkness with the seed of transformation nurtured within. The honorable ideals of the warrior may remain pure to be reborn again when all else is burned away.

Returning with awareness is also essential. The dissociated or "sleeping" memories must be integrated to become whole. Remember the stages of the hero's journey as described by Joseph Campbell; departure, initiation, and return. These must be conscious stages. The client, having passed through the hypnotic exposure, is now conscious of all that has occurred. The feelings of being cut off and alone from those who have remained behind alienate our warriors from a "social" return to friends and loved ones. The veteran as warrior/hero has entered an unfamiliar realm. This initiation represents death to the old self or old life. If they have allowed dissociation to prevent awakening, then the veteran has become like Rip Van Winkle, lost in the nightmare "sleep" of PTSD. The veteran left behind the familiar territory of past education, family, and social learning. The entry into the "wild" or "mythical" world of war is often so terrible that conscious awareness, integration, and acceptance is refused in favor of the numbness or slumber (dissociative state). The symptoms of PTSD are the signal that it is time to awaken and return to life. However, some return like the myth of Rip Van Winkle, wandering into their past like a stranger in a strange land. When the veterans fully recall the shattered knowledge of the trauma, they are awakened. The emotions that were aroused, the body sensations of the physical event, and the memories all create a sense of wholeness. The veteran may then piece together the fragments of consciousness created by the trauma into integrated wholeness.

Coming awake is difficult. Normal life after war is strange. Old relationships must be renewed with new habits and new ways. People do not like it when their loved ones change. They need to adjust to the new veteran, the changed person. The veteran warrior must learn to find safety. Our veterans must drop the defenses that have served them so well. After completing the treatment, this should be much easier. It is appropriate to tell those who care, "I have been through an ordeal and I am not the same. This has been a powerful change. I may appear a stranger but the "old me" is still a part of the "new me". The suffering I have witnessed and experienced has made me stronger and wiser." This is much better than the avoidance or excuses that lead to more difficulties. Those were false and this is true.

The veteran may have been very angry. The anger can be used to draw out the warrior, not the violent warrior, but instead the person who takes on the edge of noble honor. This is the person who has discovered previously unknown power. Our veteran must own this power in order to transcend the self, in order to promote a mission or higher good for the next stage in life. This is essential to the healthy warrior's return. Controlled anger is strength, the strength needed to change.

Yet, love is the emotion we must return to full power, love of self and other. The love of archetypal justice and what is considered right and good must be returned. This will bring the warrior home. Self discipline was the hallmark of military training. This discipline can turn anger to will and setting new goals. And, with the power of spiritual discipline, love becomes the force to transcend the evil that the warrior may have found within themselves during war.

The stories of heroes relate this struggle. The Biblical story of Jesus tells of his struggle for forty days and nights in the desert. He struggled in the garden before his crucifixion. Muhammad wrestled in a desert cave with the spirit of Allah. Buddha determined to sit beneath the Bo tree until his demons gave way. The warrior has his time to struggle with inner demons and doubt, also. But, just as the warrior was faithful to his mission, his faithfulness can now be used with love to recall his true goals, values, feelings, and beliefs. Our warriors may integrate with faith into their true selves.

So ask your clients to ponder the favorite stories of heroes and myths they recall. Allow them to imagine what it would mean to fully live those values and ideals. Explain how the warrior/ hero energy can be useful to recover a fully integrated self. The clients may list the ways that an honorable homecoming could appear. They might formulate a plan (ritual) for the honorable expression of their personal warrior energy in the future. Once again, they may return to a place where self reliance and self esteem begin to grow. This is the final task, after which, true healing is certain. Then, traumatic strength, not stress becomes the new narrative of our survivor's life.

Integration is a natural process of the unconscious mind where relationships are returned or pieced together like a puzzle that creates a picture of healing. The images of healing are the images of the warrior, father, mother, sister, brother, friend, hero, and family. These images of wholeness need to be imagined and returned to their place in our warrior's psyche. This may be guided imagery, journaling, or conversation. The end will be the same. The final work is finding the images that are right for our warrior to feel whole again. The veteran may need to explore a future type of war making that is creative and not destructive. This represents a creative undoing of the destruction of the past. Our veteran may return to a sense of duty to something beyond the self. This new sense of energy, courage, and decisiveness may result in a new, peaceful warrior. Hypnosis can be used to facilitate the process of seeking new images for life. The unconscious contains the future as well as past. Now that our clients are ready to move forward in dedication to living, they have the ability to show traumatic strength and growth. They create new meaning in life and a new future.

References

Acierno, R., Kilpatrick, D. G., Resnick, H. S., Saigh, P. A., & Bremner, J. D. (1999). Posttraumatic stress disorder in adults relative to criminal victimization: Prevalence, risk factors, and comorbidity. In *Posttraumatic stress disorder: A comprehensive text (pp. 44-68).* Needham Heights, MA: Allyn & Bacon.

Ali, T., Dunmore, E., Clark, D., & Ehlers, A. (2002). The role of negative beliefs in posttraumatic stress disorder: A comparison of assault victims and non victims. *Behavioural and Cognitive Psychotherapy, 30*(3), 249-257.

Bandler, R. (1985). *Using Your Brain for a Change.* Moab: Real People Press.

Bremner, J. D. (2002). *Does stress damage the brain?: Understanding trauma-related disorders from a mind-body perspective.* New York, NY: W W Norton & Co.

Brende, J. O., & McCann, I. L. (1984). Regressive experiences in Vietnam veterans: Their relationship to war, post-traumatic symptoms and recovery. *Journal of Contemporary Psychotherapy, 14*(1), 57-75.

Brende, J. O. (1983). A psychodynamic view of character pathology in Vietnam combat veterans. *Bulletin of the Menninger Clinic, 47*(3), 193-216.

Brende, J. O., & Benedict, B. D. (1980). The Vietnam Combat Delayed Stress Response Syndrome: Hypnotherapy of 'dissociative symptoms.' *American Journal of Clinical Hypnosis, 23*(1), 34-40.

Brewin, C. R., & Holmes, E. A. (2003). Psychological theories of posttraumatic stress disorder. *Clinical Psychology Review, 23*(3), 339-376.

Brewin, C. R. (2005). Risk factor effect sizes in PTSD: What this means for intervention. *Journal of Trauma & Dissociation, 6*(2), 123-130.

Cardena, E., Maldonado, J., van der Hart, O., Spiegel, D., Foa, E. B., Keane, T. M., et al. (2000). Hypnosis. In *Effective treatments for PTSD: Practice Guidelines from the International Society for Traumatic Stress Studies.* (pp. 350-353): Guilford Press.

Congressional Research Service Report for Congress on Estimates of Civilian Casualties. (2008). Estimates of Civilian Casualty Statistics. Available from Federation of American Scientists Web Site, http://www.fas.org/sgp/crs/mideast/RS22537.pdf)

Department of Defense, Personnel & Procurement Statistics. (2008). Personnel and Military Casualty Statistics [U.S. Military Casualties-OIF & OEF Combined] Available from DoD Statistical Information Analysis Division Web Site, http://siadapp.dmdc.osd.mil/personnel/CASUALTY/castop.htm.

Ehlers, A., & Clark, D. M. (2000). A cognitive model of posttraumatic stress disorder. *Behaviour Research and Therapy, 38*(4), 319-345.

Ehlers, A., & Clark, D. M. (2003). Early psychological interventions for adult survivors of trauma: A review. *Biological Psychiatry, 53*(9), 817-826.

Ehlers, A., Clark, D. M., Hackmann, A., McManus, F., & Fennell, M. (2005). Cognitive therapy for post-traumatic stress disorder: Development and evaluation. *Behaviour Research and Therapy, 43*(4), 413-431.

Feeny, N. C., Hembree, E. A., & Zoellner, L. A. (2003). *Myths regarding exposure therapy for PTSD.* Cognitive and Behavioral Practice, *10*(1), *85-90.*

Foa, E. B., & Rothbaum, B. O. (1998). *Treating the trauma of rape: Cognitive-behavioral therapy for PTSD. New York,* NY: *Guilford Press.*

Foa, E. B., Keane, T. M., & Friedman, M. J. (2000). *Effective treatments for PTSD: Practice Guidelines from the International Society for Traumatic Stress Studies*. New York, NY: Guilford Press.

Foa, E. B., Rothbaum, B. O., & Furr, J. M. (2003). Augmenting exposure therapy with other CBT procedures. *Psychiatric Annals, 33*(1), *47-53.*

Foa, E. B., Hembree, E. A., & Rothbaum, B. O. (2007). *Prolonged exposure therapy for PTSD: Emotional processing of traumatic experiences: Therapist guide.* New York, NY: Oxford University Press.

Freud, S. (1972). War-induced neuroses, shock treatment, and psychoanalysis. *Psyche: Zeitschrift fÃ¼r Psychoanalyse und ihre Anwendungen, 26*(12), 939-951.

Freud, S., & Horowitz, M. J. (1999). Introduction to Psycho-Analysis and the War Neuroses. In *Essential Papers on Posttraumatic Stress Disorder.* (pp. 99-106). New York, NY: New York University Press.

Hembree, E. A., Rauch, S. A. M., & Foa, E. B. (2003). *Beyond the manual: The insider's guide to prolonged exposure therapy for PTSD.* Cognitive and Behavioral Practice, *10*(1), *22-30.*

House Veteran's Affairs Committee Report. (2008). Roundtable Discussion on Issues Concerning Our Veterans["Personality Disorder": A Deliberate Misdiagnosis To Avoid Veterans' Health Care Costs!]. Available from House Committee on Veteran's Affairs Web Site, http://veterans.house.gov/news/PRArticle.aspx?NewsID=111.

Jung, C.G. (1966). *The Practice of Psychotherapy: Essays on the Psychology of the Transference and Other Subjects. (Bollingen Series 20.)* Princeton, NJ: Princeton University Press.

Kessler, R.C., Sonnega, A., Bromet, E., Hughes, M., & Nelson, C.B. (1995). Post Traumatic Stress Disorder in the National Comorbidity Survey. *Archives of General Psychiatry, 52,* 1048-1060.

Kilpatrick, D., Koenen, K., Ruggiero, K., Acierno, R., Galea, S., Resnick, H., John Roitzsch, J., Boyle, J., & Gelernter, J. (2007). The serotonin transporter genotype and social support and moderation of posttraumatic stress disorder and depression in hurricane-exposed adults. *American Journal of Psychiatry, 164*(11), 1693-1699.

Kulka, R., Schlenger, W., Fairbank, J., Hough, R., Jordan, B., Marmar, C., & Weiss, D. (1990). *Trauma and the Vietnam War generation: Report of findings from the National Vietnam Veterans Readjustment Study*. Philadelphia, PA: Brunner/Mazel.

Matsakis, A. (1994). *Post Traumatic Stress Disorder: A Complete Treatment Guide*. Oakland, CA: New Harbinger Publications.

McNally, R. J., Bryant, R.A., & Ehlers, A. . (2003). Does early psychological intervention promote recovery from posttraumatic stress. *Psychological Science in the Public Interest, 4*, 45-79.

Miller, W.R. & Rollnick, S. (2002). *Motivational Interviewing: Preparing People for Change (2nd ed.)*. New York: Guliford Press.

Nagy, Gregory. (1979). *The Best of the Achaeans: Concepts of the Hero in Archaic Greek Poetry*. Baltimore, MD: Johns Hopkins University Press.

Ouimette, P., & Brown, P. J. (2003). *Trauma and substance abuse: Causes, consequences, and treatment of comorbid disorders*. Washington, DC, US: American Psychological Association.

Phillips, M., & Frederick, C. (1995). *Healing the divided self: Clinical and Ericksonian hypnotherapy for post-traumatic and dissociative conditions*: New York: W W Norton & Co.

Pitman, R. K., Altman, B., Greenwald, E., & Longpre, R. E. (1991). Psychiatric complications during flooding therapy for posttraumatic stress disorder. *Journal of Clinical Psychiatry, 52*(1), 17-20.

Pizarro, J., Silver, R. C., & Prause, J. (2006). Physical and mental health costs of traumatic war experiences among Civil War veterans. *Archives of General Psychiatry, 63*(2), 193-200.

Rothbaum, B. O., Foa, E. B., & Hembree, E. A. (2007). *Reclaiming your life from a traumatic experience: Workbook*. New York, NY: Oxford University Press.

Shay, J. (1994) *Achilles in Vietnam: Combat Trauma and the Undoing of Character*. New York, NY: Macmillan Publishing.

Shay, J. (2002) *Odysseus in America: Combat Trauma and the Trials of Homecoming*. New York, NY: Scribner Publishing.

Spiegel, D., Hunt, T., & Dondershine, H. E. (1988). Dissociation and hypnotizability in posttraumatic stress disorder. *American Journal of Psychiatry, 145*(3), 301-305.

Spiegel, D., Rhue, J. W., Lynn, S. J., & Kirsch, I. (1993). Hypnosis in the treatment of posttraumatic stress disorders. In *Handbook of clinical hypnosis.* (pp. 493-508). Washington, DC: American Psychological Association.

Watkins, J.G. (1949). *Hypnotherapy of War Neurosis*. New York, NY: Ronald Press.

Williams, M. B., & Sommer, J. F., Jr. (2002). *Simple and complex post-traumatic stress disorder: Strategies for comprehensive treatment in clinical practice*. Binghamton, NY: Haworth Maltreatment and Trauma Press/The Haworth Press.

Wilson, J. P., Friedman, M. J., & Lindy, J. D. (2001). *Treating psychological trauma and PTSD*. New York, NY: Guilford Press.

Appendix 1

Basic Hypnotic Induction

Shift your body into a comfortable position. Separate your hands and feet so that nothing is crossed. Let yourself begin to relax completely. Let yourself feel a peaceful easiness surround you like a warm glow. You may begin to be more aware of your own thoughts and sensations. That's okay. Treat them like clouds drifting in a clear blue sky. Acknowledge them and let them drift on. In a clear blue sky. A sky that goes on forever blue. Take a long slow deep breath. Hold it for a second, then exhale slowly and easily, closing the eyes as you do so. Feel your whole body going into a state of rest. Breathe deeply again and let it out the same way. Experience your body gently becoming more and more at ease. You can be aware of the chair (couch, etc.) beneath you. You can be aware of sensations. That's right. You will notice sounds around you. And you can relax, can you not? I wonder if you ever, found yourself someplace that was so pleasant and peaceful. A happy memory. Or a dream of a place. Where it is so comfortable and safe. It is easy.......to relax. Everything can relax now and can relax later. So, allow yourself to imagine that safe comfortable place. Somewhere in nature or someplace you simply create within yourself. Relax, brighten up the colors, and notice how clear the details can be and how good it feels there. Notice anything moving. Both near and far away. Feel how peaceful and wonderful the mood can be. Perhaps the sound of the music will become more and more relaxing. Perhaps the sound of my voice will become more and more relaxing. Any sounds that don't seem to belong here will just be signals to relax more and more completely. You might feel the warmth from the light in the sky or a cool delicate breeze. So the temperature is just perfect. You may detect familiar calming odors. The clouds continue to drift across the sky....the sky that goes on forever... and a golden white light shines down between the clouds. Just like a light from heaven. Caressing you and allowing you to feel warm and relaxed...warm and relaxed. Imagine this light stands for everything good in life. Peace, love, tranquility, and pure sweet relaxation.

Imagine this light surrounding you and flowing through you. Allow it to simply flow through you from head to toe relaxing every cell, muscle, and tissue. As it flows from head to toe, it will warm and relax each and every part of you. It begins at the top of your head and flows into your forehead. Feel the forehead becoming warm and relaxed. It gently moves down to the eyes. Think about the eyes relaxing. All the tiny muscles that move the eyes becoming warm and relaxed, going loose, limp and at ease. As the eyes get a little heavier and heavier. As your eyes relax, your whole body responds by going even deeper into this peaceful relaxed state. Giving yourself the gift of relaxation. Feel this energy of peace move through your face and allow some space between your teeth as the cheeks and jaw muscles relax. Moving to a pleasant state of rest. Flooding your brain through each and every cell with wonderful peaceful relaxing energy. Feel this sensation of healing and relaxing flow from your brain to every cell in your body. Notice the light flowing down the back of the head, neck, and shoulders. Warming and relaxing. Soothing the neck and shoulders in a wonderful way as gravity pulls your shoulders down into their natural comfortable position automatically. Your mind may wander and drift, wander and drift or become drowsy...foggy. What ever happens is completely natural. You will still hear the relaxing sounds of the music. You will still hear the relaxing sound of my voice like a comfortable feeling in the background. Words blend into one another and flow to your subconscious naturally. So you are free, free from having to listen because your mind will easily and automatically record their meanings anyway. And your mind can simply unwind, relax, and let go. Let go. As the world turns and the sun rises on each new day, each day is similar and each day is unique with lessons of its own for us to learn. Regardless of the ups/downs, moods, stresses, of day to day life, they have nothing to do with this. Fears, guilts, blames, problems, and pressures are useless here and unnecessary. This is just pure relaxation. Allow the light to continue to flow. Moving down through the arms. Feel the relaxing warmth flow down through the upper arms, warm & relaxed, down through the elbows, flowing through the forearms, warm & relaxed, down through the wrists, hands, and flowing out through the fingertips taking with it all tension or tightness so the arms are pleasantly loose, limp, loose, and limp. You may feel some tingling in the fingers that shows how easily you are becoming relaxed and at ease. Notice the breathing becoming a bit deeper and with each relaxing breath feel the warm relaxing energy flow easing you deeper and even deeper into relaxation. Experience the light flowing down through the torso, down through the back, down every single vertebrae radiating out to every single muscle so that the back becomes deeply warmed and relaxed, settling into a natural comfortable position automatically. Flowing through all of your internal organs, allowing them to be washed in this golden white light, your heart, lungs, liver, kidneys, stomach, genitals all receive the relaxing, healing light. All of your organs released into this blissful state of pure relaxation. Feel the light continue to flow, down through your hips and bottom, warm and relaxed, down through your thighs, swirling through your knees with sweet warmth and release, down through your calves, your ankles, your feet, warm and relaxed, and out through your toes taking with it all tension or tightness that may have been locked up in your body and is useless to you now. Feel the sensations in your body begin to dim just like dimming the lights. And with each beat of your heart, allow yourself to go deeper, deeper, deeper, deeper into relaxation (slowing rhythm). All of the muscles and tendons of the body go loose and limp, loose and limp and at ease. (Use deepening techniques if needed).

Revivification induction script for returning clients

This induction is brief. It follows the assumption that once our clients have experienced trance and practiced relaxation at home, they will be easily returned to the trance state.

Shift your body into a comfortable position. Let yourself begin to relax completely. Let yourself feel a peaceful easiness surround you like a warm glow. You may begin to be more aware of your own thoughts or sensations in an arm or leg. You can be aware of the cushions you relax against. Notice your breath as it moves gently in and out. Take a long slow deep breath, closing the eyes as you do so. Feel your whole body going into a state of rest. Breathe deeply again and let it out the same way. Experience your body gently becoming more and more at ease. That's right. You will notice sounds around you. And you can relax, can you not? As you relax, listening to the sound of my voice, you may begin to remember, the experiences of relaxation, of trance, that you have had before. How it felt then. To listen, as you began to drift down. The feeling in your hands, or legs, or arms. That feeling of relaxation. The alterations in your awareness, as you became more and more comfortable. More and more at ease. In that comfortable, safe place. Enjoying the opportunity, to allow the body to relax. Everything to relax. As trance continues, as you drift deeper…and deeper… More ……and more at ease. Very good. And as your drift deeper, my voice drifts with you. Becoming part of the experience. Relaxing, ….drifting down ….letting go …. Allowing thoughts to drift…….images to appear…. Needing to do nothing at all. …drifting easily and effortlessly into that peaceful, safe place…..of deep………

deep...........comfort.......that's right. (Use deepening techniques if needed).

Trauma scripts:

Abreaction Approach

"You are in a comfortable, safe, and relaxed place now. Imagine vividly the feelings you have described that are distressing for you. Locate the feeling and allow yourself to return to the first time you felt it."

If needed –

"I am going to count from one to three. Simply allow your mind to wander and drift back through time. When I reach the number three, you will find yourself at the time and place where these feelings began. One, ... following the feeling, drifting gently back to its source. Two, ...leaving now behind, floating back over time. And three, ...You have returned to the source of these feelings."

- "What are you aware of?"
- "What happens next?"
- "What are you experiencing?"
- "What might be important for you to remember now?"

Directive Approach

"I am going to count from one to three and when I reach the number three you will find that you have returned to (whatever the event). One ..... your mind is drifting into the past (pause). Two, moving further back and more relaxed. And, three, you are now there and can recall the entire experience."

(Continue with questions above).

Non-Directive (seeking) Approach

"Imagine a direction that your mind may travel to retrieve memories. Possibly, there is a line that extends from the present into the past or forward to the future. This would be your timeline. Allow yourself to drift free now. Drifting free of here and now. Allow your mind to drift towards the past. We are going to return to the event that has been causing your distress. I will count from one to three and when I reach the number three you will return to the memory you need to understand your current situation. One, floating back in time (pause). Two, drifting to the exact place and time you need to be aware of for your recovery. Three, drifting to the source of your distress, NOW." (Continue with open questions).

Appendix 2

Motivational Handouts and Forms

To be used with clients who appear unmotivated towards therapy in order to enhance motivation to change. These may also be used to create directive scripts for change.

CURRENT VS. FUTURE LIFESTYLES :

Your lifestyle can affect your health (physical and mental), finances, relationships, and achievements. To examine your lifestyle NOW, please complete the following timeline describing your daily activities on a "typical day." Remember to include times when you might be involved in activities or behaviors you wish to change. Then answer the questions.

7am ______________________ 5pm ______________________

8am ______________________ 6pm ______________________

9am ______________________ 7pm ______________________

10am ______________________ 8pm ______________________

11am ______________________ 9pm ______________________

Noon ______________________ 10pm ______________________

1pm ______________________ 11pm ______________________

2pm ______________________ Midnight ______________________

3pm ______________________ 1am ______________________

4pm ______________________ 2am + ______________________

1. What do you like or enjoy the most about your lifestyle?

2. What about your lifestyle is not so good or causes you difficulty?

3. How are your health, finances, relationships, and achievements?

4. How could things be better? What would have to change?

What are the benefits and costs of maintaining my current behavior?

Benefits of remaining the same	Costs of remaining the same

Health –	**Health –**
Relationships –	**Relationships –**
Financial -	**Financial -**
Other-	**Other-**

What are the benefits and costs of change?

Benefits of Changing?	Costs of Changing?
Health –	Health –
Relationships –	Relationships –
Financial -	Financial -
Other-	Other-

WHAT IS IMPORTANT TO ME:

Everyone has things they believe in, standards to live by, or values. However, sometimes we act in ways that do not protect the things we value most or match our values. We may be tired, distracted by other things, or forgetful. Take some time here to remember your values and record them.

1. What are some of your strong personal beliefs and values? For example, some people believe strongly in being honest, assisting others, or helping their families. What are some things that you believe make a person a "good" person, son/daughter, mother/father, friend, or student? If you could be the best "you" you could be what qualities would you have.

Make a list here of values/traits or actions that you believe are most meaningful and important, then circle the two you feel are most essential to you right now. You may want to number them so that you put them in order of importance.

2. Is there anything that is getting in the way of your living by these standards? What may stand in the way of your being the best you can be? What would have to change for you to live more closely by your most important values and beliefs?

FUTURE INTENTION:

"Night & Day dream of what you intend to do, and what you intend to be, and those dreams will interpret your intentions, let no doubt enter your intentions" - Dr. Wayne Dyer

Hold an Image of the life you want in mind and that image will become reality.

Often it is helpful to take the time to look ahead in our lives. Having an intention or a mental picture of how we would like things to be in the future can help us to feel less anxious, help us to maintain direction/focus, and help us to plan our time to move closer to our hopes and dreams. We **always** move in the direction of our most dominant thinking.

1. What are your hopes, intentions, and dreams for the future? Be specific. Fill in the details. Imagine you can have anything you want for yourself. What would that be?

2. What are things you can do **less of** to make these intentions a reality?

What other things would you like to become involved in that would be helpful to replace the time spent on less helpful actions/ behaviors?

3. What are you doing and can you do **more of beginning now** in your life to help you make these intentions reality? What new things would you like to become involved in?

<u>I AM SUCCESSFUL</u>:

Sometimes we get disheartened when we forget the times that we have been successful at making changes in our lives or achieving something we wanted very much. <u>Everyone has been successful</u> at making changes in their life at some point or time. If you are alive, you had a successful birth. Let's use this exercise to remember your personal successes.

1. List some positive changes you have made in your life.

2. <u>Pick one</u> of the changes you listed above, maybe the one that was hardest to accomplish or that you feel most proud of, and list the following:

a. When did you start thinking about making the change? What was happening in your life at the time?

b. Did you make the change all at once or take small steps?

c. What did you do all at once or what were the steps?

d. How do you feel about the change today?

Sometimes we forget how powerful we can be if we need to. Let's look at the ways in which we are personally strong and powerful.

1. List your personal strengths and strong points:

2. How can these traits assist you in making changes in your life?

3. What could hinder your progress towards change?

4. How will your strengths help remove obstacles to your future?

Handouts and Forms for Subjective Distress and Intake Interview

On the following pages you will find forms for both the client and the therapist to record subjective distress scores. You will also find an intake outline with complete questions to cover any intake for PTSD.

Appendix 3

In Vivo Exposure Hierarchy

Name: ______________________________

Date: ______________________________

Therapist: ______________________________

SDS Anchor Points – In order to make the SDS scale fit your life, we will need to establish some anchor points. In what situation lately have you felt NO discomfort? Please enter this at zero. When have you been most distressed? Enter that at 10. Now based on these answers, what would be a 5 for you? Use these numbers to rate other events.

0 - ______________________________

5 - ______________________________

10 - ______________________________

Item	**SDS (Sess. 2)**	**SDS (Final Sess.)**
1. ______________________	______	______
2. ______________________	______	______
3. ______________________	______	______
4. ______________________	______	______
5. ______________________	______	______
6. ______________________	______	______
7. ______________________	______	______
8. ______________________	______	______
9. ______________________	______	______
10. ______________________	______	______
11. ______________________	______	______
12. ______________________	______	______
13. ______________________	______	______
14. ______________________	______	______
15. ______________________	______	______

Therapist Hypnotic Exposure Recording Form

Name of Client: ______________________________

Therapist: ______________________________

Date: __________ Exposure #: __________ Session #: __________

Description of exposure in imagination: __________

____

____

____

____

Start time	SDS	Notes
Beginning	______	______________________
10 minutes	______	______________________
20 minutes	______	______________________
30 minutes	______	______________________
40 minutes	______	______________________
50 minutes	______	______________________
60 minutes	______	______________________

Therapist Intake Interview for Hypnotic Treatment of PTSD_ (Session 1)

Client: ______________________________ Date: ________

Therapist: ____

Client age: _____ Educational level: _______Date of Birth: ______

Race:___________Marital Status: ______ Work status: ________

Current employment:_________________________________

Current reported difficulties or Psychiatric Diagnosis: _________

____

____

____

Any other current treatments/treatment professionals: ________

____

____

____

SAY TO CLIENT: I am going to ask you some questions about the trauma and how you have been doing or feeling lately, since the trauma. This may be difficult but it is necessary. If there is anything I can do to help you feel more comfortable please let me know. Do you have any questions for me before we start? Tell me all you remember about the trauma and how it is affecting you? _

____

____

____

____

Sometimes people experience other traumas. Has this happened to you? Have you ever witnessed or experienced other traumatic events before this?________________________________

What will be the primary focus of this treatment (target)? Which of all the things that have happened to you bothers you the most?

When it was happening did you think you would be killed or seriously hurt? Yes No

Did you feel helpless, horrified, or terrified? Yes No

Where exactly did this occur (describe)? ____________________

What physical injuries did you have? Have these continued to be a problem? ________________________________

What type of medical attention did you receive? Was it helpful? Are you still under medical care? ________________________

Who is to blame for the trauma? How so?

Have you been feeling guilty about the trauma? Shamed? Angry?

What health issues do you have lately? Are they related to the trauma?

How has your mood been? What things are you enjoying doing?

Since the trauma, have you ever felt that life is not worth living or thought about suicide? Have you made a serious suicide attempt since the trauma? Do you have a plan now?

Have you ever deliberately hurt your self in any way? How and when?

Have you been hospitalized since the trauma for any mental health, emotional, or nervous condition? Why and when were you hospitalized?

Summarize current risk assessment :

Alcohol & Drug Use: Current prescriptions:

Street Drugs:

Over the Counter medications:

____

____

____

____

____

Alcohol Use (quantity & frequency of use): ________________

____

____

____

____

____

Is there anything else you feel I need to know about your PTSD that I have not asked about? ____________________________

____

____

____

____

Other Books by Transpersonal Publishing

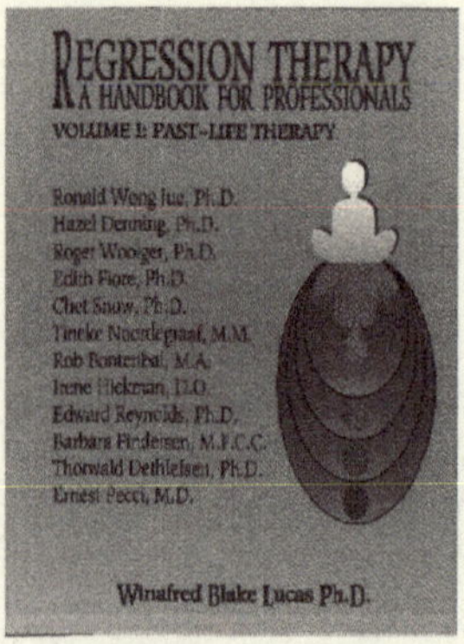

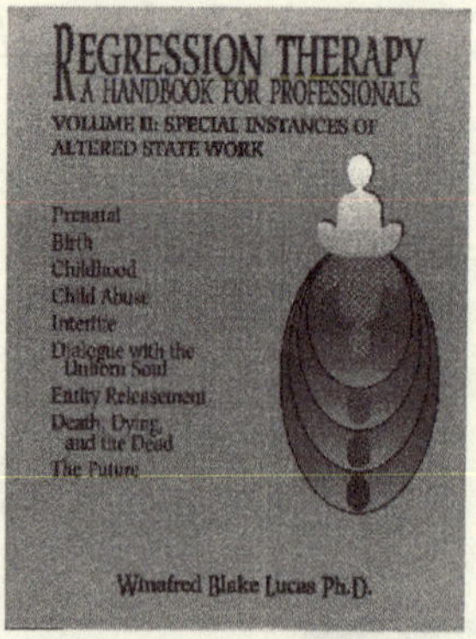

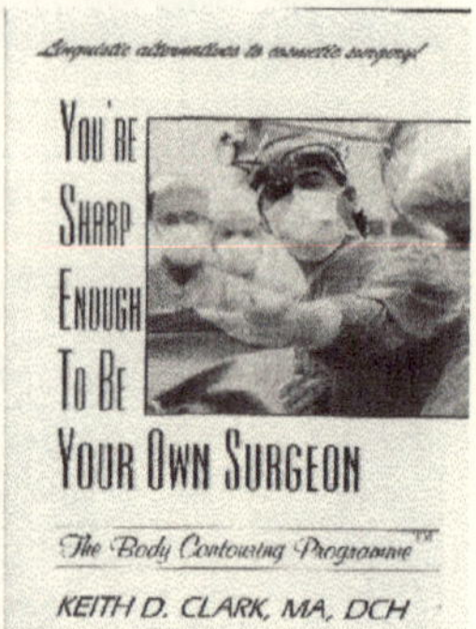

To see these and other books by the publisher, go to:
www.TranspersonalPublishing.com

Michael McGee, LPC, MA, DCH

Michael McGee has a Doctorate in Clinical Hypnotherapy, a Master's Degree in Counseling Psychology and is a Licensed Professional Counselor with a private practice in Southwest Virginia.

He is a member of the **American Society of Clinical Hypnosis**, the **International Medical & Dental Hypnotherapy Association**, and the **National Association of Transpersonal Hypnotherapy** including specialized training for weight loss hypnosis, smoking cessation hypnosis, hypnoanesthesia, and hypnotic regression. His Doctorate Dissertation researched treating PTSD with hypnosis is the basis for this publication.

He is an accomplished presenter and has contributed programs for the **American Society of Clinical Hypnosis, National Association of Transpersonal Hypnotherapy**, and **Creative Alternatives in Therapy Conferences** sponsored by Radford University for the past nine years. These include presentations such as, PTSD treatment, Motivational Interviewing, Cognitive Hypnotherapy, Integrating Spirituality into Counseling, Modern Culture and Relapse Prevention, and Adolescents & Archetypes – Transpersonal Therapeutic Approaches.

Since 1999, he has taught various courses in Psychology at a small liberal arts university where he educated multiple sections combined of Abnormal Psychology, Adolescent Psychology, Child -Developmental Psychology, Introduction to Psychology, Personality, and Social Psychology.